DARE TO BE

For a complete list of Management Books 2000 titles,
visit our web-site on http://www.mb2000.com

DARE TO BE DIFFERENT

How to create business advantage through innovation and unique selling propositions

Alessandro Forte

First edition published in 2005

Thid new edition published in 2008 by Management Books 2000 Ltd
Forge House, Limes Road
Kemble, Cirencester
Gloucestershire, GL7 6AD, UK
Tel: 01285 771441
Fax: 01285 771055
E-mail: info@mb2000.com
Web: www.mb2000.com

British Library Cataloguing in Publication Data is available

ISBN 9781852526047

Contents

About the Author

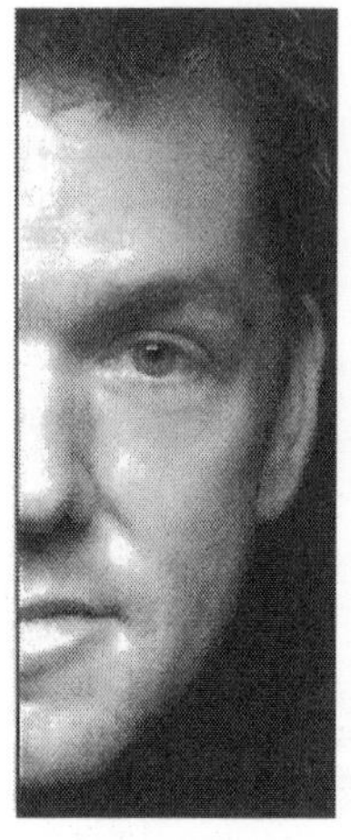

Sandro (as he prefers to be known) was born in 1968, the eldest of four children to Leo, a successful restaurateur, and Carol. During a fairly ordinary education he had, at various times, decided to be a doctor, teacher, actor and policeman. By the time he left a three-year university and drama school degree course, he was only certain about one thing – he had to find a way to pay off his student overdraft.

His determination to do so took him back to his home town of Weston-super-Mare where a chance meeting with a family friend, who had just started his own financial consultancy practice, took him into the life insurance business.

After getting nowhere fast, Sandro decided to move from an administrative role to one that involved selling; something completely new to him. Starting out with no more than twelve contacts, he took nearly three years to make anything like a decent living. By then, however, he had spent a considerable amount of time studying the books and tapes from most of the good business practitioners and suddenly he was qualifying for Million Dollar Round Table (MDRT) Top Of The Table; MDRT being the premier organisation for life insurance people and the organisation's Top Of The Table representing the top 0.25% of insurance sales people in the World.

His unprecedented success as a salesman led to invitations to speak at Life Insurance Association meetings around the United Kingdom and then, more significantly, at their 2000 Annual Convention in London. Many other invitations followed including the prestigious Main Platform at MDRT and from other sales and business organisations from as far afield as Malaysia, South Africa, Singapore, Canada, Israel, Philippines, Thailand, Vietnam, Taiwan and India.

Now regarded as one of the great 'new age' business practitioners and speakers, Sandro is in considerable demand to share his innovative, yet simple and transferable, ideas with others.

His hobbies include golf, football, travelling and the theatre. What spare time he has is spent with his wife Ruth and twin children Thomas and Ellie.

Foreword

In 1976, when I was just seven years old, my dad – who was a wonderful, caring man – was diagnosed with lung cancer. It was terminal. I was only a small boy at the time so I didn't understand the horrors my father would face as he fought the disease.

Sadly, he passed away two years later. He left my mum and four children – I was the eldest. During his life, he had built up an excellent restaurant business. We lived in a big house and wanted for nothing. But under the terms of a family agreement, the business passed to his sister; my mum was left with the house but, significantly, no other financial provision. It was inevitable she couldn't afford to run the house and, within two years, it was sold to pay mounting debts and the five of us were moved into welfare housing – a two-bedroomed property.

As sometimes happens, when one door closes in life, another seems to open and, shortly after, my mum met Dave, an equally lovely man whom I came to think of as my own father. But during the time I was growing up, I had always promised myself I would never let my family go through the same experience again, so, when I came into the life insurance business in 1989, I had the opportunity to ensure there was money available for the family if the worst happened; if lightning were to strike twice.

How many times have we put off approaching someone for fear of rejection – especially rejection from someone we love? For two years, I put it off. My own parents needed life insurance – the number of children had now grown to seven – but I found myself guilty of procrastinating, pre-determining what they would say if I approached them.

Could lightning strike twice? Of course I hoped not, but could I really stand back and watch my mother go through the same thing again if it did?

I'd promised myself that I would see this one through, to at least talk to them about the cover I knew they needed. I was then 24 years old but the youngest of the seven children was only 3. The first thing Dave said was they could never afford the premiums and there were plenty of other things they'd rather be doing with what little money they had. For once, I didn't walk away from a 'knock-back' but simply suggested we submit a proposal to see what terms were offered. A little reluctantly Dave agreed, although he said he wasn't promising anything.

In truth, I think he liked the idea of a free medical – but during tests was found to have diabetes. He wasn't far off being uninsurable but I managed to get terms – a 300% premium increase and then attempted to explain to them there was now even more reason to invest in the insurance because insurance companies don't tend to increase premiums unless there is an increased need for cover. But at three times the premium, I knew I might be fighting a lost cause. Of course, I worried about them affording the premiums but, after much discussion, they agreed. They agreed because they knew what the financial implications would be if lightning did strike twice. I'd kept my promise but, more than anything else, I'd done the right thing. I knew my mum could now sleep just a bit easier at night …

Then our world fell apart

Only two months after taking out the policy Dave fell ill – he was diagnosed with stomach cancer. I couldn't believe it was happening to us again. This time, though, the cancer was very progressive. It had apparently been there for some time masked, ironically, by the symptoms of the diabetes. There was to be no two-year battle for him. Within a week he was in hospital and just four days later he was dying. As I sat alone by his bedside one day, he was drifting in and out of consciousness. Finally, with failing strength, he whispered to me, 'Son, thank you for what you did for your family. I'm so proud of you.' Those were the last words he ever spoke.

In many ways I'm lucky. I realise that's not the sort of thing you might expect me to say but it's true. If I could turn back time, I would, of course. But I can't. So I'm left to reflect on whether I would actually have what I have now if things had been different. Would I still be in the financial services business? Unlikely. Would I have two beautiful children? Probably not. Fate is a strange thing.

Sometimes, a profoundly tragic experience like the one I suffered – along with the rest of my family – can have a positive impact on one's life. For me, that manifested itself as a focus and determination to succeed, starting with telling everyone I could about what had

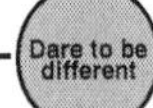

happened to us and, in the process, encouraging them to take positive action in dealing with their own financial affairs.

This book isn't just about my 'story'. After all, many people have endured similar experiences. Rather, it is about the practical application of a number of ideas which transformed a very ordinary business (I had spent quite a few years in the business 'wilderness') into something creative and highly successful. The insurance policy I sold to my parents meant that my mother, now married for a third time, has the financial security I have always tried to advocate.

I'm very proud to have been asked to share these ideas; both to audiences around the world and now in the form of a book.

I have been thinking about this book for some time but it was only when I got asked on the several hundredth occasion whether I was going to commit my sales and business ideas to text, that I set the goal and started writing.

Now that I have done what I set out to do, I have the opportunity to publicly thank some of the (many) people who have made this book possible.

Firstly I want to thank my parents – all of them; including my aunt – for the sacrifices they made and the unwavering support they gave me during some rather 'colourful' formative years. To the Metcalfes, Moggs and the Isaacs – good friends who always keep me smiling. To the many people who helped me put this book together; not least my long suffering Personal Assistant who has been with me almost from the beginning and who never seemed to get fed up with all the re-writes and corrections. To my wife Ruth for her love, support and encouragement – even during the difficult times.

I also want to thank the many people whose ideas I have used to good effect and to the vast number of friends I have made around the world; not least Tony Gordon – one of the true greats of the Life Insurance business and who was so kind to me in helping me develop my speaking engagements.

Lastly, I want to thank you for investing in this book. I hope that, as a result of reading it, you feel inspired enough to take the action that will undoubtedly make a difference to your life and the lives of others.

Dedication

This book is dedicated to my wife Ruth and our children, Thomas and Ellie, with all my love.

1

The Most Extraordinary Fact We Choose to Ignore

Imagine being born with a blindfold on. You're brought up by your parents with this artificial impediment and knowing no different, you never remove it. In fact, you're forbidden to take it off ... and there it stays for years until you finally get used to it. So used to it, that you now depend on it being there, and if someone came along and suggested you dispense with it, you'd recoil at the very idea.

Then one day your worst fears are realised. Through an accident, the blindfold is ripped away from your eyes. For the first time, you allow pure light to strike the back of your eyes. You start to see pictures and images – the like of which you've never viewed before. It's frightening, yet exciting – and in a short period of time you're living a brand new life in a brand new world wondering how stupid you were all those years to deprive yourself of the gift of sight, not to mention how ignorant your parents were to allow it all in the first place.

A strange story you may be thinking, and yet this is an analogy for something very real that happens to over ninety percent of all people born into our world of abundant opportunity.

Of the ten percent who take a different approach and remove the blindfold of their own volition, only three percent actually do something constructive as a result, the people who really make the grade ... ***who dare to be different.***

The remaining seven percent who got close will live out the rest of their lives knowing that they should have taken some important action steps but since they didn't know what these steps were, they remain sighted yet look at the blindfold in their hands, rather than at the world out there – buzzing with possibilities.

Right now I know two things about you. First, that you are part of the ten percent group. You have to be, otherwise you would not have bought this book. You've taken off the blindfold either recently or maybe quite some time ago.

The second fact I know about you is that you're also part of the seven percent group who aspires to be in the top three percent, yet you're not completely clear how to go about it and what steps to take in what order. It's why you're reading this book right now.

Like all the 'seven percenters', you're searching for answers, and possibly will continue to search – maybe for the rest of your life – never quite finding the key to the lock the door marked 'Ultimate Success'.

And this is precisely why I've written this book. I'm searching for like-minded souls who would benefit from having a set of steps to help them get closer to opening that door and achieving whatever 'ultimate success' means to them.

By the way, that's the bit to which only you know the answer because I cannot define 'ultimate success' for you. Which brings me to the heart of the matter. *The most extraordinary fact we choose to ignore.*

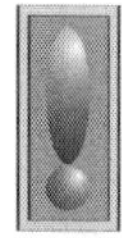

We live in an ever-changing environment and nothing changes more than life itself. To cope with this change and to capitalise on it, we must, above all else, be *consistent* and *persistent.*

Read on for powerful ideas on these two factors.

Some of the technological advances in recent years have been staggering. In a split second, we can now communicate with pretty much anyone, anywhere, on the planet. We can buy most goods and services via a computer. Thanks to the development of medical practice we are now living longer, we're better educated than at any

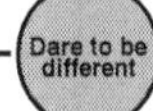

other time in our history and we're building bigger cities and business developments.

Of course this hasn't happened overnight. The process of change has been with us since time began. It's the nature of who we are and what we are here to do, yet almost inevitably we find change such a tough nut to crack. It's so easy to say, 'we should embrace change', and yet as we all know, it's easier said than done. Change is tough, but by being able to deal with it – surf the wave rather than get demolished by its power – you don't just become a survivor, you become a success story.

Success and change are interlinked. Change in essence is noticing what isn't working in any given situation, working out what will probably work better, trying it out, making adjustments until it works well, then looking at something else in your life that doesn't work and going through the same process.

Sounds so simple. So what's stopping you?

If you were to look at a room of successful people as I have at 'Top of the Table', during Million Dollar Round Table meetings, where you have a gathering of the crème de la crème in financial services, and look for a common trait, to begin with it appears an impossible task.

Looking more closely at the gathering however, I'm aware that it isn't about what we as a group *knew* but about what we *do* and *have done*. The actions we're prepared to take – daily, monthly, annually …and in a word, consistently.

Do anything positive consistently and you can't help but become a runaway success story. Remove consistency and you end up with mediocrity, excuses and falsehoods, all of which are linked with failure. And some of the biggest successes ever were of course failures once upon a time. However it was their determination to be successful by using consistency that separated them from the crowd.

Consider this: think of something you've achieved in the past. Did consistency play a part? If you didn't keep 'keeping on', would you still have achieved it? Consistency can be a short burst or long haul, but it's normally about doing the things you least want to do, and the things that other people downright refuse to do even though they know in their hearts that they should be doing it.

I'm going to suggest that mastering 'ultimate success' is based on four things:

- **Understanding the nature and art of being consistent.**
- **Being able to deflect any thought that's likely to make you stop being consistent.**
- **Having 'inside' knowledge around the best tools and techniques needed to make being consistent easy to achieve.**
- **Having an all-consuming passion to be consistent about your primary goal. This is often the number one reason why you're alive.**

The reason most people never unlock their true potential is because being mediocre is often perceived as easier than achieving great success.

After all, it's easier to avoid taking action than to drop some excuse we've invented not to perform. Think of the person trying to win a one-hundred metre sprint with a ball and chain attached to one foot. It's almost impossible to win but yet most people would not want to be released from their constraint because it is more comfortable running at the back, with an excuse you can clearly show to the world. Success as you know is not a matter of chance but a matter of choice.

Have you heard of these well-known inspirational questions?

'What great thing would you attempt if you could not fail?'

'What is the greatest goal you could possibly imagine yourself achieving?'

I ask because it's important we know, right from the start, what our **Primary Goal** is. Note that it's singular not plural. I am referring to one life goal that captures under its umbrella, all the other smaller goals.

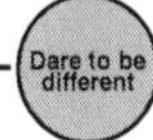

For me, my Primary Goal was originally… to spend an average of three days a week looking after a small, select number of clients, and to spend the other two days a week speaking, lecturing or writing, and enjoying long weekends with my family.

Surprisingly, if my goal was simply to make a lot of money, it's extremely unlikely I would have fulfilled my ambitions so fast. The first goal is specific and credible where the second is unspecified and creates a number of unanswered questions. Naturally my current Primary Goal is based on my original, however it's adjusted for the future. It's unhealthy not to have a current, ongoing Primary Goal. Didn't someone once say, 'Success is a journey, not a destination'?

Looking at another element in the list of four requirements to 'Ultimate Success' we need to fully understand **thought and action.**

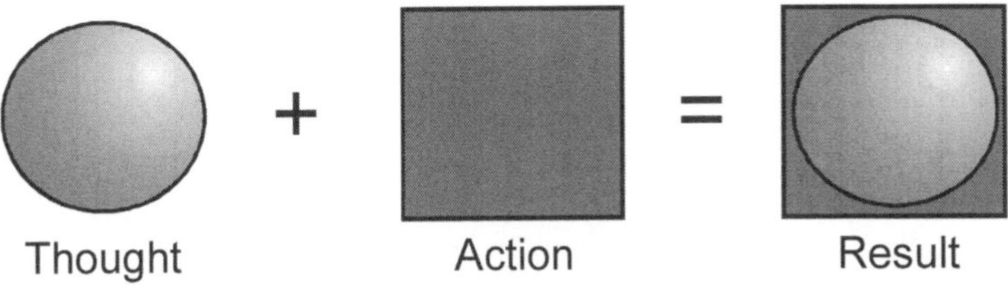

Occasionally, the process breaks down because something stops us taking action. It's something called **interference** and it can take many forms.

When we get distracted as we inevitably do from time to time, a thought however good, remains just that – a thought. So we need to be aware of the things that sometimes hold us back. Once we are aware of them, we stand a much greater chance of eliminating them for good. More about this in a later chapter.

In research in the USA in the eighties around success and failure, something fascinating was discovered. Eighty-eight percent of people are not afraid of failure but of success. On the face of it, it makes no sense. How can it be that most people who seem to desire success so much, are also afraid of attaining it? And yet the twelve percent that fear failure more than success tend to already be infinitely more successful than the eighty-eight percent group.

Ask yourself a question:

'What is it about being more successful that actually scares you?'

I asked this question of a mediocre salesperson who wanted some coaching tips from me. Her response was interesting. She said, *'I would be afraid that once I had made the grade and become successful, I'd have to keep doing it every year – and that I find scary.'*

Actually, what she was saying is that she preferred never to be successful, not even for one year, than succeed and plan her way to continue the journey with delight and excitement which is more likely to follow a really successful breakthrough, in my opinion.

My consulting firm, Forte Global Consulting, was set up to help people from all professions, businesses, industries and backgrounds to truly improve performance and succeed *without fear*. Naturally we get some very large, well-known companies that our senior partners have worked with over the years requesting help with sales teams. Yet it all boils down to the four premises I listed earlier. So, on to a major tool I'd like to start by sharing.

It's an idea I've used to great effect for many years. In fact, I should go so far as to say it has been one of the biggest contributing factors to the rapid business and financial success I have achieved and enjoyed in a relatively short space of time. It's called **MindChangers**.

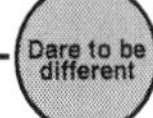

MindChangers

These are a set of tools that emerged from the world's number one business associated with winning – the World of Sports. Sports coaches and psychologists down the ages have contributed in creating a tool kit that can be used by anyone to dramatically change their results.

These tools include *Flip Cards, The Star, The Lift, The Train, Image Diary* and *Fast Forward* to name but a few. Without exception, any world-class athlete will admit to using at least one of the above on a regular basis.

There's a chapter on MindChangers coming up which will bring you up to speed. However, let's give you a taste of what's involved.

> I'd like you to talk to yourself. In a moment, set this book aside and talk to yourself. If you can be overheard and fear a white van pulling up with two men carrying a straitjacket – just remember that you are only verbalising what you always do! Everyone, without exception, talks to themselves – normally in silence in their minds. So I'd like you to chat away to yourself about the year ahead. Talk about what you expect to achieve. Do this now for a couple of minutes before reading on …

How did you get on? Was it easy? Motivating? Inspirational? Okay, a question for you. Did you use the present tense, past tense or future tense? In other words did you say, 'I am doing …' 'I will do …' or 'I did …'

The chances are you used the future and maybe the present tense, and neglected the past tense because it had not happened yet. And here's the point of the MindChanger tool called *Fast Forward.*

> This time, I want you to do the same thing but assume it's a year into the future and you're looking back, reminding yourself what's already happened – as if it has. So put the book down and do this again but now talk in the past tense …

How did it feel? For most people it's very different, more motivating and yet initially less comfortable. (Remember what I said about change – discomfort and success inextricably being linked).

This technique is a favourite with top football and rugby teams, tennis players and athletes. I once saw this being demonstrated with a top UK-based football team. Players talked about 'next Saturday's big game'. They discussed in precise detail how they watched it happening, who had passed the ball to whom, how it had been passed, what happened after that and who had scored the goal. They did it time and time again discussing it *in the past tense* as if it had already happened. I then witnessed the game in real time and was staggered as I watched what was discussed actually happen before my very eyes. It was strange yet extremely exciting – feelings which were also carried on the faces of the players; players who were in fact less excited about scoring the goal than they were about emulating their strategy and executing it perfectly.

If you were to do fast forward regularly – and it's more fun with someone else – you would start to change your beliefs automatically. I promise you, whether you initially believed them or not, after 28 days, you'd start to believe them anyway. What we believe, our minds tend to see. Believing is seeing – not the other way around. In order to see the result, use MindChangers … the simplest of which is Fast Forward.

'Isn't it amazing how I keep exceeding my sales target by 50%!'

Also, you can do something similar by writing on cards. Whilst I do not profess to be a psychologist, I do know that the subconscious mind is infinitely more powerful than the conscious mind. After all, we walk, talk, breathe and recall certain information at will – without having to think about what we're doing. So, let's imagine we could commit our goals, ambitions and dreams to our subconscious – what then? MindChangers are now used by most of the people I have ever

consulted or coached and I've witnessed some incredible results. Who in their right mind wouldn't want to give them a go? A tool kit with a proven track record.

I had a goal to buy a top of the range Mercedes in 1996. I read the statement, along with sixty-two others, every day before I went to my office and in every case habits started to form, without my necessarily being aware of them.

Remarkably, I would find myself telephoning the Mercedes dealership without a particular reason and discussing the car I was going to purchase, describing it in detail. Actually, this happened regularly and yet, apart from a brief glance at my MindChangers each morning, I hadn't really given much thought to how the purchase of a Mercedes was going to happen, especially knowing that I was on a fifteen-month waiting list …

Every time I called the showroom, I'd end up describing a different feature of the car and then, amazingly, going out that day and writing more business than normal. I'd also convinced myself I was going to purchase it for cash on another MindChanger flip card.

Then one day, out of the blue, I had a call. It was the Mercedes salesman with whom I had, by now, struck up a firm friendship. He told me that he had a cancelled order from the owner of a business who was in financial difficulty. Because I had so accurately described my 'dream' car and because it so closely matched the cancelled order, he had called me straight away to avoid the struggle of finding another prospective purchaser on his fifteen-month waiting list.

Was it luck or fate that contrived to ensure I achieved my goal? Or did I have a direct hand in this? Some friends smile and say it was a pure coincidence but I do know that the MindChangers did fire me up without question – at least enough to convince the salesman to choose me from his long list and, in doing so, helped me achieve my goal. Incidentally, also 'by coincidence', I then had the cash available to pay for it.

Eventually, I suppose, I would have taken delivery of a brand new sports car. But there's a big difference between those who wait for their opportunities and those who go out and take them. Since I became a 'taker', I get many, many happy coincidences happening to me.

Let's summarise our journey so far

Understand your life goal

It's vital to understand what single outcome we're ultimately looking to achieve. Mine was initially around freedom from a 9-5 job. Our Primary Goal should be the focus around which we hang all our other performance goals.

Develop performance goals

Once you know what you are trying to achieve, consider the things you need to do to help achieve the outcome. Commit your goals to your subconscious by using 'MindChangers'.

React positively to success

As the great Mehdi Fakharadzeh says in his book *'Nothing Is Impossible'* – our limits are set only by ourselves. Why not approach life and business with total confidence? It's so much more fun and rewarding!

Be aware of interference

Beware of that little voice that constantly chats to you in your head. If it's negative and adversely challenging your goals and dreams, control it before it consumes you. Again, your MindChanger Tool Kit would be useful here.

Maintain balance

Always plan with a strong 'work-life balance' in your mind. Work effectively, play hard. If you plan this at the outset, it's most likely to happen.

Love change

If changes are needed, take positive action. Taking the first steps does not necessarily involve a change of strategy. It could all be about a change of heart which relates to belief and attitude.

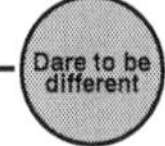

Have consistency in everything you choose to do

If it's worth doing, be consistent about it. Also take action. It's **thought plus action** that will get you the desired results you so richly deserve.

So, this all-important chapter is about:

☞ **Consistency + Persistence = Basis of success**

Consistency then is often the extraordinary fact we choose to ignore. If you think of any successful individual, particularly someone who has made the grade on their own over a period of time, you'll know that they've been *consistent in their approach* and *persistent in their resolve*. These two factors joined together have created the basis of their initial success and the levels of success they've enjoyed thereafter.

Being **consistent** means knowing what new habits you have to create and activate on a regular daily basis. Being **persistent** means whenever you fall over, stand up, dust yourself off and go for it again.

> I remember once watching two martial artists having a bout of judo. One was a black belt, a man of about thirty, and his opponent was his pupil of around twenty. In this full bout, naturally the older black belt was winning just about every throw and the younger green belt was finding himself on the mat time and time again. However, it was the green belt that impressed me more than the more experienced black belt. The reason was that the green belt would immediately get to his feet as soon as his body touched the mat. There was no pause, no quick intake of breath, just getting up, standing and facing his opponent with the resolve of a future champion.

When you are this way with your goals and are prepared to persist until you attain what it is you are passionate about in life, you will always succeed.

The most extraordinary factor we choose to ignore then is this formula around consistency and persistence. You now may choose to acknowledge it and use it to your advantage or completely set it aside and miss its power and enormous potential.

End-of-chapter classic quotes

'Great people are just ordinary people with an extraordinary amount of determination.'

'The best partnerships do not come from a 50/50 effort. They come from a 100% effort by both parties – unconditionally.'

*'Children don't spell LOVE, L-O-V-E:
They spell LOVE, T-I-M-E!'*

'It always seems impossible – until it's done.'

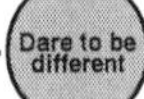

ACTION STEPS

Taking action

Before you move onto the next chapter, I ask you to complete the following exercises. Without a commitment – whether you succeed or fail is immaterial at this stage – you will not progress. So, please, give them a go.

1. **Write down your Primary Goal.**

2. **Write down a list of your other goals – short, medium and long-term.**

3. **Commit at least 10 of these goals to MindChanger flip cards and read them briefly each day. Create one MindChanger flipcard for every goal.**

4. **Copy the following onto a sheet of paper and score yourself based on where you are right now. 1 is low, 10 is high. We'll review your progress later in the book:**

a. Self-confidence
b. Personal ambitions
c. Adapting to change
d. Persistence
e. Taking action
f. Order and organisation
g. Communication (with others)
h. Personal appearance
i Plans and planning
j. Time management
k. Daily activity awareness
l. Focus
m. Dealing with problems
n. Happiness and personal contentment
o. Physical condition/ achievement
p. Sales

WARNING! Procrastination will cost you dearly. Complete these before you move to Chapter 2.

2

The Key to the Door

Getting the key to the door – and running a successful practice is the subject of this chapter. In building a strong financial services practice, do you want lots of clients or a few really good ones?' There's no right or wrong answer here and I can't answer this for you.

Whichever you choose, there are benefits and challenges. With lots of clients, you are making the field you sow very fertile, with immense opportunity to harvest your crops each and every month. The challenge is that there's more work involved with this option.

Equally, I once knew of a top adviser who had merely fourteen clients, all multi-millionaires who he would probably see once a month. At least once a year he'd do business with each client … which is all he needed to ensure he had a very healthy annual turnover. Of course, the danger lies in losing a few of these clients for whatever reason – meaning a dramatic difference to income.

The second question to getting the key to the door of business opportunity is to ask yourself whether you want to make prospecting – the art of casting your net – easy or difficult. You may think this is a silly question because you'll surely want to make it easy. Curious then isn't it, how many financial advisers there are who clearly haven't asked themselves this question – given they make life so difficult for themselves. Personally, I love prospecting but freely admit that the more successful I get, the less I have to do it!

The secret of making prospecting easy comes from three areas – sources I believe you need to establish if you haven't already done so.

- The first source of business involves creating a system which

runs itself linked to your Top Twenty Clients. I say twenty, but the number is up to you.

- Second, you need to identify a group of professional introducers. I mean lawyers, accountants, bankers and the like.
- Finally create and develop your very own 'Marketing Engine'.

With these three elements in place, prospecting becomes a simpler, regular and highly profitable process.

Your Top Twenty

As a matter of course, I ensure all my clients know what is expected of them. This is naturally done with great subtlety, yet I am very 'up front' about it and do it with the utmost integrity.

If you are straight with people, they are equally straight with you. This way you can quickly identify those clients who you can later rely on to recommend you from time to time. If this is done through clients who are already quite wealthy, they will introduce you to people like themselves – provided you are specific about what you want.

The process is to mention the fact you work largely from personal introductions, as a throwaway line, at the first meeting.

> 'I'm not sure if I've already mentioned this, Michael, but I make it a professional business practice to work from personal introductions, and the reason I get so many from my new clients is because I like to think I do a first-class job for all of them ...'

Now move on swiftly to something else. In the second meeting come back to the subject.

> 'I think I mentioned last time that I make it a professional business practice to work from personal introductions. In your case, Michael, who would you recommend I speak with?'

What's staggering … is that this 'process' is ridiculously simple to execute. I advise you to practise the words until they roll off your tongue, then use them with every new client. However, if you use this *consistently* you are likely to get a very full diary, so don't say I didn't warn you!

Professional introducers

I was once making a formal presentation as guest speaker to a large group of successful financial advisers in the USA. One delegate came up to me with a smile and said, 'Of course it must help to be in a country where it's easy to work with other professionals'. I paused and considered what he was inferring. He repeated his belief again from a different angle. 'What makes you think that?' I asked. 'Because it's true. Here in the States it's not so easy. We are not viewed in the same way as financial advisers are in other countries like the UK.'

I was fascinated. I looked at the guy's expression and could tell how weighed down he was by this belief, which of course to me wasn't true at all ! In fact, early on in my career, I had numerous colleagues share with me their 'paradigms' of how America is the easiest place to sell life assurance – followed by their mistaken belief as to why.

We all carry paradigms around in our heads – that fixed pattern or model belief, core to our thinking on a particular subject. Early paradigms in history include the world being flat and the universe revolving around our planet – indeed, people were actually put to death for daring to suggest otherwise.

In financial services, there is a whole array of paradigms, the majority of which relate either to prospecting for new business or gaining more business from existing clients. Let's smash a couple right now before we go any further!

'It's hard to get professional introductions.'

It's actually the easiest thing in the world – provided there is no

legislation to stop you and you have made a good case to the professional about who you are, how you do business and what conceivable benefit there is to their clients as well as to themselves.

'It's embarrassing to ask for introductions from friends.'

If you know what to say to your friends, they will be constantly calling you with opportunities.

Think about the last really amazing movie you saw – one that impressed you by the story, action – or both. One I thought was great was *The Sixth Sense*. I can't remember how many friends I mentioned it to and I told them all I'd watched it a few times, such was its impact on me.

Now, no one paid me for the 'marketing' that I decided to do for the makers of this hit movie. I wanted to because I knew I would get good feedback from everyone I recommended it to; people coming back to me saying, 'Sandro, what a great movie! Thanks for telling me …' How many times have you done the same thing, enjoying the buzz of the praise you get for a good recommendation?

At a convention in Toronto, Canada, I met an adviser whose paradigm was, *'never ever sell to your friends; always keep your friends and clients separate'*. I am not sure where this came from, but I asked him to imagine going to the funeral of a good friend only to realise their family was now in extreme financial difficulty because he failed to at least talk to his friend about what he did.

Creating a **Marketing Engine** is something I will briefly deal with shortly, after I introduce you to an amazing tool. It has not only worked for me but many other financial advisers since I was first introduced to it by my former business coach and mentor Glen McCoy, who created the Dynamic Phone Path in the 1980s.

The Dynamic Phone Path

Getting the first meeting with your prospect should actually be easy because they will hopefully have come from a strong personal recommendation from a friend or introducer.

However, you still may have to make the odd 'cold call'; whether it's through a first-time contact with a personal introduction or because you wish to build bridges with a new source of business.

May I say that before you use something like this, it's much easier to sit with your friend or introducer, *hand them your mobile phone and get them to make the initial call while you are there in person.* Just ask them to introduce your name – no more – and then pass the phone back to you. This relates to another astonishing paradigm. Most financial advisers think this idea is not workable because few advisers deal with personal introductions this way. Why they insist on taking a name and phone number as a personal introduction and then go back to their office and – in a less advantageous position – make the call which will be relatively cold! Madness or what?

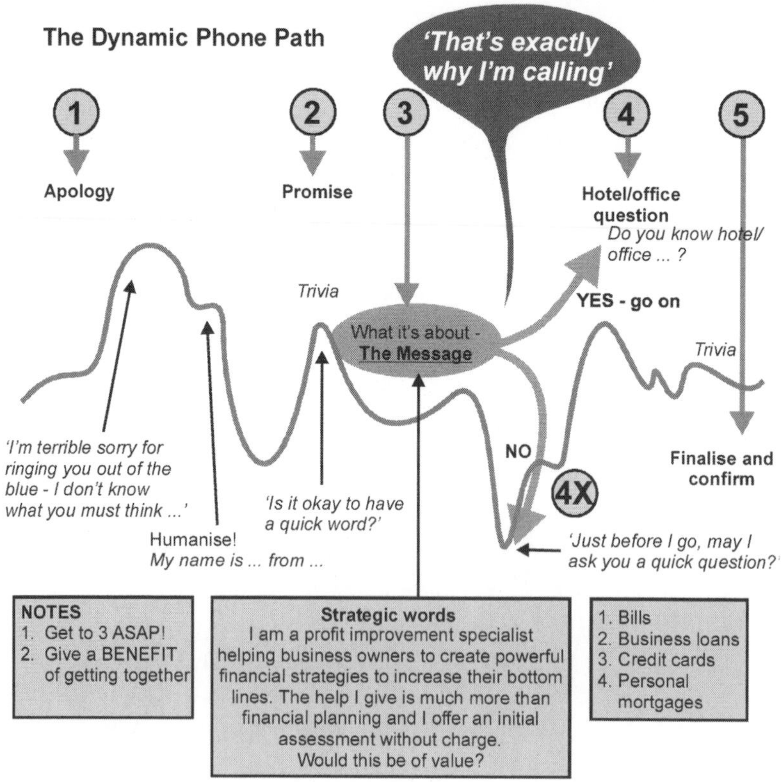

The Dynamic Phone Path

'That's exactly why I'm calling'

1 Apology

2 Promise

3

4 Hotel/office question

5

Do you know hotel/ office ... ?

Trivia

What it's about - **The Message**

YES - go on

Trivia

NO

4X

Finalise and confirm

'I'm terrible sorry for ringing you out of the blue - I don't know what you must think ...'

Humanise!
My name is ... from ...

'Is it okay to have a quick word?'

'Just before I go, may I ask you a quick question?'

NOTES
1. Get to 3 ASAP!
2. Give a BENEFIT of getting together

Strategic words
I am a profit improvement specialist helping business owners to create powerful financial strategies to increase their bottom lines. The help I give is much more than financial planning and I offer an initial assessment without charge.
Would this be of value?

1. Bills
2. Business loans
3. Credit cards
4. Personal mortgages

Every call, regardless of who it's to or who is involved, has a set of dynamics. I can tell a poorly conceived sales call a mile off. The person speaks in a formal, somewhat unnatural way, in almost a staccato voice and keeps using my surname more than they should. They ask impertinent questions and can come across as patronising or arrogant.

The Dynamic Phone Path helps to eliminate all of this by linking a suggested set of dynamics to an outbound call.

How it all works is simple. Place your finger on the line at point 1 and work through to point 6.

The apology (step 1)

To start with an apology needs to be completely **genuine**. The majority of people attempting to sell to me on the phone completely overlook this critical factor by brushing it over with a surly, 'Sorry to trouble you'. Simply by the tone of their voice, I know they're not sorry one little bit! This immediately puts me on my guard.

So how about this:

Hello, is that Michael? Michael Turner?
(Yes)
Hello ... I'm so very sorry to be ringing you out of the blue like this.
(Who is it?)
My name is Sandro, Sandro Forte from The Forte Group. Is this a good time to speak with you?
(Yes)
(No)

Okay, so let's look at what we have here. Notice how you use the prospect's first name first followed by his or her full name. This is a way of subconsciously asking their permission to be on first name terms. Equally, when I say who I am, I use the same technique.

I cannot stress enough how important it is to practise this on friends and family and only when they say it sounds truly genuine can you then be sure you've got your delivery right.

Where a person indicates that particular moment is not a good time to speak, agree a time when it is. If they want to know what it's about, mention the person who gave you their details and some important information they may want to know about. However, the person you are calling cannot have it both ways … they cannot expect to know what the call is about and then be too busy to speak to you! Refrain from falling in this trap!

Someone once said to me that using the words, 'I am so very sorry for ringing you out of the blue' is a lie. I completely disagree. Why should it be a lie? You are calling the person out of the blue unless of course they were waiting for you to call?

It's important to apologise before introducing yourself by name and company – not after. The apology cushions the introduction and makes it 65% more likely they will continue to want to communicate with you after they know who you are.

So far so good.

Now for step 2, the promise

> I've recently taken on Mary West as a client and your name came up in conversation a couple of times, hence **the promise** to call to offer you my help, given I make it a professional business practice to work with the friends and families of my clients before anyone else.

The thing about the word 'promise' is that its inclusion reflects upon the user. It says something about you. Maybe that you like to keep your word and take trust and integrity seriously. People warm to people like that. Once more, the statement is based on fact, not fiction. I will have used the word when the prospect's details were given to me. I would have replied to say, via an e-mail to the introducer, 'Thank you for your kind introduction … I do promise to get in touch with Michael as soon as possible.'

I'd also like to add that it's important to humanise the conversation, not formalise it. Talk to the person as you would to an old friend, not as if you are speaking to a complete stranger. This, naturally, will make you sound less like the stereotypical salesperson.

So to 'The Message', step 3 – your core reason for the call

The difficulty most advisers face is knowing what to say in order to get the prospect to 'first base' and an agreement to an initial exploratory meeting. Say too much and they make excuses, say too little and they get suspicious and cynical. So, the best way I believe is to have a powerful statement which serves as your 'hook' to capture their attention and hopefully open their mind at the same time.

> 'I am a profit improvement specialist helping business owners create powerful financial strategies to increase their bottom lines. The help I give is much more than financial planning and I offer an initial assessment without charge. Would this be of value?'

A message for non-business prospects could be:

> 'I am currently helping individuals to improve their personal wealth in ways which realise more disposable income. Would more funds for you to spend or retain as you choose be useful?'

It's useful to note the phrase – *'That's exactly why I am calling'* when faced with any objection.

Example:

> 'I've got no time to meet you at the moment ...'
>
> 'That's exactly why I'm calling! Most of my clients have much more quality time now their finances support them properly ... would having more time be of value?'

Step 4

Step 4 takes us to the 'Hotel or Office' question, if you immediately go on to it. After dealing with any objection, it works especially well.

'Do you know the Marriot Hotel in the city?' or 'Do you know the Axis Office building?'

In asking this question, you are moving the person to discussing meeting up by using the question as 'a spine' in your approach.

(Yes I do...)

'May I suggest we meet there next week so that I may have the opportunity of introducing myself and sharing some beneficial ideas – as I have already done with your friend Mary? What time of the day suits you best?

Sometimes you'll hit a brick wall. They are simply not interested for whatever reason. So use step 4X.

'Just before I go.....May I ask you a quick question?'

Normally people say yes to this – if only to get rid of you!

You must pay a lot of money out on bills ...? If it were possible to reduce these bills permanently, would that be of value?'

When using the Phone Path, do also call existing clients, friends and contacts purely for social reasons. Always tell them how well things are going for you and how many clients you are helping. These calls break up the calls to new prospects (because you can guarantee you will not be rejected!) which keeps you positive and mentally flexible and invariably you'll pick up new business from speaking to the people you know so well.

The first meeting

First impressions are everything ... but so are second impressions. Fail to create a clean, professional image and you'll undoubtedly struggle to win your client's trust and confidence further down the

track. People cannot help but look at you and analyse – either consciously or subconsciously – your attire, your body language, gestures, the state of your briefcase or computer bag and so on.

It should also go without saying that you need to be punctual. Yet so few sales people get this simple courtesy mastered. Usually, the advisers who are always late have a poor attitude towards time mastery. This can be easily corrected by following the guidance notes in Chapter 4.

Even if we do get to our client on time, we need to appear smart and well groomed. I despair of the advisers who smell of alcohol, tobacco or, unbelievably, body odour!

Turning up in an ill-fitting suit or with dirty shoes sends out completely the wrong message. I appreciate that a new wardrobe of clothes might be a bit extreme, but one or two clean smart outfits will give your clients more confidence in your abilities as a sales professional.

Another thing often overlooked is the use of a decent writing implement. No client I know – especially the chief executive of a large company – is going to be that impressed if you were to suddenly produce a disposable pen from your pocket in order to take notes or complete an application form. Again, I'm not suggesting a huge investment in such an accessory, but something that looks reasonably professional will definitely get noticed.

There are many parts to building good impressions. Double check you are up to scratch by looking in the mirror before leaving for an appointment and ask yourself the question, 'Would I buy from myself?'

Nothing will be achieved by blitzing our prospect with the benefit of our technical knowledge, however good it may be. Neither is there anything to be gained by going straight into a perfectly-rehearsed sales script. The quickest and most effective way of establishing trust – the most fundamental of all building blocks in any relationship – is to spend time selling yourself.

Without fail, I always spend five or ten minutes sharing information on my business, what we do, our philosophies and our professional working practices. During my introduction, I explain how we differ from other firms of advisers and talk about what makes us unique.

The reason for this is simple. Firstly, I want to build rapport and then I want my clients to like and trust me. I want them to have confidence in my commitment and ability to serve them well.

Secondly I want to be sure I sell value, not price. Selling price is the most certain way to business failure because you can be sure that if you don't already work in a business sector where the same product can be obtained at the same price almost anywhere else, then someone will always find a way to undercut you.

So I talk about what else I can bring to the client over and above the creation of a sound financial portfolio designed to create wealth.

Once I have handed over my business card and Terms of Business (this is a simple document designed to confirm my status as an adviser – whether 'tied' or independent etc) I will say the following:

> 'Do you mind if I just spend five or ten minutes telling you a little about me and my business?
>
> I have been in financial services for sixteen years, the last ten running my own private practice. The business was built on some key principles, not least that we look to build long-term relationships with our clients.
>
> We are one of the few financial services businesses of its kind to have a written Client Service Charter which outlines the way we go about building those relationships. Every client is treated in an honest, ethical and professional manner and we respond to telephone calls and letters within given time frames or pay a financial penalty to a charity of your choice.
>
> Fortunately, we don't get caught out too often, but when we do, you can be sure we will be striving to ensure the same mistake never happens again.
>
> Most significantly of all, we work with a number of business partners – for example solicitors, accountants, stockbrokers, mortgage brokers and general insurance brokers.
>
> This allows you to access a full range of services with one

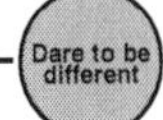

telephone call. If you have your own family solicitor or accountant, then we'd be only too pleased to work with them.

But for those people who don't, I'm sure you can see the benefit of accessing all the services you will might need, from time to time, under one roof?

The more services you use, the greater the discounts – because we can use our 'buying power' as a company to negotiate on your behalf. So, for example, if you arrange your mortgage through us, we can recommend the services of a solicitor with whom we have negotiated a discounted fee for the legal work, often amounting to a significant saving.

In addition, we can offer discounted home insurance, saving you more money.

I have a number of other ideas that could save you considerable amounts of money. If you can just tell me a little about you, I'll pick up on this again. Is that OK?'

It's important to get your prospect saying 'Yes' right from the start. Does your prospect want to save time? Of course. Does your prospect want to save money? Yes, definitely. Does your prospect want to provide for his or her financial future? Without doubt.

Consider, for a moment, the introductory 'script' I use with my prospects. I believe it encapsulates everything I want and need to say at this early stage in the relationship. I mention, openly, the things they will undoubtedly want from an adviser – trust, honesty, professionalism and a long-term relationship.

When prospective clients start to talk about themselves, I usually just jot down notes on a piece of paper. I find that few people I have only just met feel comfortable with a formal question and answer session at this early stage – in order to get a 'Fact Find' completed. It's also amazing how much more information you can gather if you keep things informal. Ask lots of 'open' questions (why, how, what, where, when, who) and, needless to say, listening is also very important at this time.

After I have all the basic information, I remind them of my promise to talk about other money-saving ideas which actually lend themselves well to the completion of the Fact Find.

So I will ask which credit card(s) they use, whom their mortgage and home insurance is with, what existing financial plans they have, whether they pay bank charges, how much they paid in legal and tax adviser fees last year and whether they have made a will.

There is, more often than not, considerable potential to save large sums of money – particularly if you have strategic alliances with other advisers who can help you put a discounted portfolio together.

Some advisers baulk at the suggestion they should 'waste' time by talking about saving money on credit cards when there is 'nothing in it' for them – but I beg to differ.

Firstly, referring them to a local bank manager with whom you have negotiated a special rate on savings accounts or credit cards – or just providing an application form for completion – takes no time at all. It's all part of value-added service. If we don't compete on service, then our businesses are almost certainly doomed to failure because, in an ever more competitive environment, we won't always be able to compete on price alone.

This also sets you apart from the vast number of advisers who can't see the point of offering services where they have no direct return financially. Such short-sighted sales people are a big help to me – because they make me look good when clients are shopping around.

End-of-chapter classic quotes

'We can achieve everything we want to achieve if only we have the courage to believe we can achieve it.'

'We should stop worrying about failure and worry about the opportunities we miss when we don't even try.'

'A big business is a small business that did the right things.'

'Don't be afraid to fail with an approach to any client or customer. After all, we have all failed at just about everything we have ever attempted: swimming; riding a bicycle; writing; speaking. What's so different now?'

'Obstacles are the things you see when you fail to focus on your goals.'

ACTION STEPS

1. If you don't already have one, design an introductory script format which you will use at every first meeting. Learn it by heart.

2. As soon as you can, buy yourself a new business outfit.

3. Make 10 calls using the Dynamic Phone Path and make every third call a social call to a friend, old client or contact.

4. Find out the best credit card, loan and mortgage offers available and carry a few application forms with you. Hand them to your clients, where appropriate. Better still, build relationships with a bank manager, lawyer, accountant and the other professionals who could add value by offering discounts on their services, without committing you to any work.

5. Call your Top Twenty clients and ask them to help you build your business by introducing you to other people like them.

3

Concept Power

When I started my career in the financial services industry, I wondered how well suited I was going to be for this new opportunity. People immediately told me I was too young and I questioned whether I was convincing enough or that I had what it took to be a success. But I soon came to realise that it's honesty, and a willingness to learn coupled with *consistency* and *perseverance* that would largely determine the level of my success.

It's great to be part of an industry that doesn't sell tangible products from shelves in a store – that you can do a sales presentation anywhere on our planet – as I have frequently done thirty-five thousand feet in the sky, sitting in first or business class – where incidentally there are often some great prospects who sometimes cannot escape for a good six hours heading west towards North America!

Frankly, I would not want to trade my profession or intangible products for anything. The fact is, you can sell a product to almost anyone if you get the concept right in your head first and then have the skill to transfer the same thought to them subtly and without any of the hard pressure sales techniques that were part of the twentieth century, no longer welcome in this new century of increasingly sophisticated prospects and clients.

So it's fantastic that our business is not about the products we sell, but ideas we have to offer the people we care about. Clients buy the idea first and then they buy you second. The old notion that people buy people first has changed in recent times. If this fact were true, people would never consider shopping around. Unfortunately you can be loved by a prospect but if a competitor has a better solution that will offer bigger and more exciting benefits – they suffer the competitor to ensure they get their hands on the right product. Think about it – have you ever hated the person or store you are buying from – yet know you can't get that product or service from anywhere else, so you buy it anyway, albeit under sufferance.

So, in financial services, we don't get paid by the hour but for the value we bring to an hour. Quoting percentages and estimated rates of growth might be something we are obliged to do as part of a professional code of conduct, but it's not what moves people to action.

For these reasons, it nearly always works best to convey things simply. Equally, trying to impress your client with how smart you are will generally not establish trust nor help the relationship-building process. After all, if your clients thought you were stupid, they wouldn't be talking to you. Education – and giving a client the benefit of that knowledge – is of course important but it's only half the equation. Transferring knowledge and ideas into robust concepts that clients can easily understand is what really works – and has done me proud over the years.

Selling your concept

It doesn't matter whether we are trying to sell to the most financially naive individual or to a rocket scientist, there are still some basics to understand.

In the days when I was in management, I remember visiting a client with one of my more experienced advisers. The first meeting had gone well and now he was back, with me as an on-looker to complete the business in the form of signed applications. In fact, we were there to present solutions for four identified requirements. There was a clear need to address life cover, income protection, pension and private medical insurance. The solutions to this client's problems were sound and the monthly premiums fitted comfortably within the stated budget. What could possibly go wrong? It was a formality – or so my colleague thought.

What he'd failed to realise was that his client was not in the least bit technically minded. Nor did she want to know about every last detail on the quotation or the vast array of paperwork that followed. She simply wanted to know what most of us want to know – what was being recommended (the product), what did it do (the benefits) and how much would it cost (the premium).

Not picking this up, the adviser proceeded to bombard the poor woman with technical detail like a hurricane. Were his efforts legally compliant? Certainly. But were they effective? Not at all.

Having sat back in his chair, confident of getting his client's agreement following this twenty-five-minute bombardment, the adviser was dumb-struck when the client suggested that she needed time to think about his recommendations.

At that point, not wanting to see a grown man cry, I leaned forward and asked the lady whether I could summarise. She seemed relieved, so I proceeded to write – on a single sheet of paper – what she was being asked to invest in, what was being recommended and the basic benefit each solution provided.

The piece of paper was divided into twelve equal segments, four rows of three, and each box contained a word or number. Within five minutes, we were completing the application forms.

Product	Benefit	Cost

This summary report, as I refer to it now, is a regular feature at my presentation meetings. I sell the concept first and offer the technical details after that.

Of course, I'm not suggesting for a moment that we fail to comply with our legal obligations to provide full product and commission disclosure or explain the quotation in detail. However, there's nothing to stop us explaining the benefits behind our recommendations before we proceed to the more technical aspects.

A single sheet of paper, set out in the way I have described above, is an extremely effective way to help our clients visualise and hence understand the rationale behind a recommendation – and it's sight of this that they buy. If the recommendation, however simple, makes sense clearly fitting their requirements and budget, then there are unlikely to be any objections.

I'm a great believer in keeping things simple. Even those who want considerable amounts of detail and technical information still want the thinking behind the advice presented in a straight-forward way.

There are many other conceptual ideas I use when I need to help a client to see how important it is to take positive action – irrespective of whether this results in a sale.

One of these ideas is something I call the 'Two Jobs' presentation. Let's assume for a moment our client currently enjoys a salary of £19,000 ($35,000) per annum and drives a company car.

I will start by taking him back to the time he was first interviewed, and accepted for the job that currently provides these benefits. I would say something like:

> 'When you first took your job, you were offered £19,000 ($35,000) a year and a company car.
>
> Presumably you're still relatively happy with the package that you received from your employer today?
>
> What I would like you to imagine is that I'm the same person who interviewed you for the job – except on this occasion I am going to offer you £18,000 ($32,500) a year and the same company car. But I'm also going to provide income protection which ensures up to 50% of your salary will continue to be paid in the event of accident, sickness or long-term illness. In addition to this, Death-in-Service cover will ensure that your family will receive a lump sum equal to three times your annual salary in the event of your demise.
>
> You'll also get a lump sum in the event of a diagnosis of cancer, heart disease, stroke or a number of other serious illnesses. In

addition to those benefits, your employer would make a contribution to a pension plan in your name and you would also be offered private medical insurance for you and your entire family.

Let me ask you this: would you still have taken this job if it had been offered? And even now, which of the two jobs do you consider to be more attractive?'

The two jobs concept

JOB A	JOB B
• £19,000 pa	• £18,000 pa
• Company car	• Income Protection (50% of salary)
	• Death in Service (3 x salary)
	• Critical Illness (2 x salary)
	• Personal pension
	• Private medical insurance
	• Company car

In twelve years, I have never yet come across a client who has told me that the first of the two job offers seemed to be worth far more than the latter. Instead, all, without exception, point to the second job offer and make the types of comments which only go to prove that the benefits – many of which would provide for their family – significantly outweigh the cost.

Bear in mind, too, that most people realise additional taxes will need to be paid on the higher salary option so the alternative job offer appears much better value for money. I would suggest this is an excellent sales concept when presenting several solutions to either an existing or prospective client because it is in a form which they can grasp instantly.

Some other conceptual ideas

1. Which of these items do you normally insure?

I find it remarkable that we as human beings, are quick to insure material items in our lives such as cars, audio and television equipment and the homes in which we live. Yet how many of us insure our pay cheques that we receive each month? I have heard many professional advisers use the question, *'If you had a machine in your cellar that, each time you turned the handle, produced £500 ($875) in legal currency...would you insure the device for breakage or malfunction?'* The answer, of course, is 'Yes'. Isn't that a bit like insuring your pay cheque with the amount produced relative to your earnings. By the way, the second question would be, *'How much would you insure it for if you cranked the handle five times a week forty-eight weeks of the year?'* The mind boggles.

Self-cancelling loans and overdrafts

Referring back to the Dynamic Phone Path, ask your corporate clients whether they have a self-cancelling loan or overdraft.

When they say no, you can advise them that for a fractional increase in the amount of their loan or rate charged on their overdraft you can see to it that the company's debts are wiped out in the event of death, disability or critical illness of any key person in the company … otherwise known as Key Person Assurance.

Puppet on a String

This is particularly good for Key Person Assurance or Shareholder Protection. Draw a puppet on a string. Ask the question, *'If you ran a puppet show who would you insure – the puppet or the person who pulls the strings?'*

Where on the Line?

X ______________________________ Y
(Min premium) (Max premium)

You have established that the minimum investment amount for the solution you're recommending is 'X' per month and that 'Y' is the maximum. Ask your client to indicate where on the line he or she would be comfortable investing each month. Invariably the mark on the line will be beyond the minimum suggestion.

Remember: The premium chosen, whatever it is – is only a small fraction of the size of the real problem and is easier to sort out than keeping the problem.

Cycling up the Hill

The analogy of cycling up a hill – the steepness of which becomes more pronounced the longer our client leaves financial planning, is one that is well known.

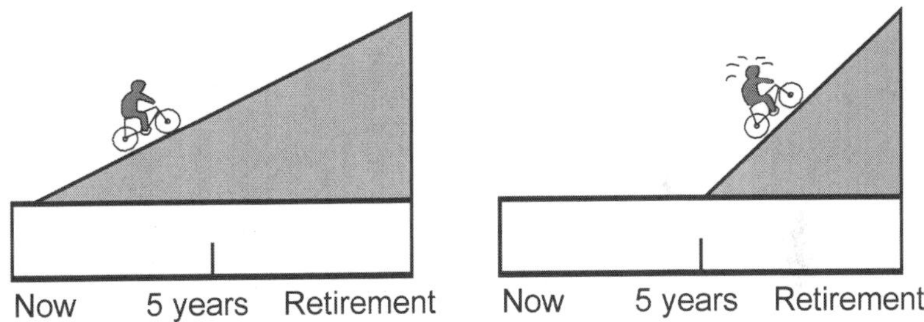

Thoughts around a hill of your own

How often do we stop to think about our own hill? I'm not necessarily talking about a sound financial plan for ourselves although I've never quite understood why some sales people have never invested in their own concepts and solutions.

I'm questioning why we make life so difficult for ourselves on occasions, leaving tasks and decision making to the last moment, avoiding doing important things, not being there for children whilst they're growing up and so on. Leaving it all too late and the hill ahead of all of us can sometimes become far too steep to negotiate – and we end up falling backwards with the inevitable pain and hardship attached.

The same applies to our business. We want to increase our productivity but somehow expect this to happen miraculously with hardly any effort. If there was a perfect number of first or second meetings that any self respecting adviser planned to achieve each week, I would suggest it is ten – on average, two a day. But with this you also need to work smarter.

So how can we stop our own hill getting steeper? I suggest a number of things:

- Eliminate unnecessary time in the office.
- Carefully plan travel routes, leaving enough time between meetings. Better still, ask your clients to visit you and offer some kind of incentive if it helps eliminate non-productive time.
- Avoid taking unnecessary calls.
- Avoid extended lunch hours and attending to personal matters in the working day – a huge temptation!
- Eliminate coffee breaks from your daily routine but do stop for a proper lunch. The 'lunch is for wimps' quote still lives in the eighties with high stress rates and record numbers of gastric ulcers.
- Move your desk away from any disruptive or negative influences. Work from home if necessary.
- Face all your personal responsibilities.

The 10% Account

This is a really simple but effective discipline which I would suggest everyone uses and is a great concept to tell all your clients about. By the way, if you are the sort of person who tells clients how to best plan their money but fails to take the same advice yourself – shame on you!

So, the idea is that whatever we earn in a salary, commission or

fees, we set ourselves a target of saving 10% of any amounts coming in – in a high-interest account that we never draw upon or spend until retirement or at the very least a rainy day. Quite apart from being a very effective savings idea, this strategy should also provide the business owner with some capital value. In effect, you pay everyone but yourself normally. How many cheque stubs do you have in your cheque book with your name on? Very few, I bet. This reverses the trend. You are paying yourself …

End-of-chapter classic quotes

'Anyone who doesn't believe in life insurance deserves to die at least once without it.'

'We are the professionals who, when tragedy strikes a family, walk through the front door with the money when everyone else is walking out of the back door with the money.'

'Nothing in the world can take the place of persistence. Talent will not; nothing is more common than unsuccessful men with talent. Genius will not; unrewarded genius is almost a proverb. Education will not; the world is full of educated derelicts. Persistence and determination alone are omnipotent.'

(To the business owner who does not value protection, saying investment in his own business is better than wasting money on insurance.) *'That's fine, but which would you rather give up to pay for the taxes and other charges when you die – your best investment or your worst investment?'*

'The highest reward for a person's toil is not what he or she gets for it but what he or she becomes by it.'

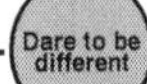

ACTION STEPS

Try something really simple to help the consistency forming process.

Use the following grid to confirm that you are taking care of the necessary disciplines in your business each day.

The items to be listed are those which require daily attention such as writing a pre-determined level of business, making telephone calls, spending time with the family, exercise, strategic planning or anything else that needs to be included.

Numbers one to seven correspond with the days of the week. Simply tick to confirm the job's been done. There's a space for comments, if this is needed, but the most important thing is to ensure that each and every day, positive action is being taken across all important business and personal disciplines. Remember any regular action that spans 28 days almost certainly will become a habit.

Item	1	2	3	4	5	6	7	Comments

4

Your Most Valuable Resource

I was speaking to a fellow passenger on a plane during a flight to one of my coaching trips in the Far East. He came across as being very successful – and he couldn't help but name-drop a few well known businesses that he had worked with, not to mention the odd famous entrepreneur he knew personally.

Yet, when I really observed his face and general demeanour, I was looking at a tired, out of shape man who clearly wasn't looking after himself. In fact, he told me that he worked a six-day week, would often get up at four in the morning and never ever got to bed before midnight. He seemed to be saying that hard work was the route to success and success equals long hours and punishing schedules.

As he spoke, I thought about my own situation. Three days a week on average, running one of the most successful financial services businesses in the world – as an individual – and having to have two days a week assigned to things I absolutely adore, namely public speaking engagements, writing, golf and going to the health club regularly.

In fact, when I indicated that my day finished at five-thirty as a rule and I never worked at weekends, I could see him judging me as a bit of a wimp and probably assuming I wasn't that successful at all.

Isn't it strange how our beliefs govern our lives? That's fine if you have a set of beliefs that support and look after you, but completely another story if they are actually making you ill over the long term and probably even shortening your life.

As humans, most of us carry around one major flaw in the belief department of our minds. We believe money is more valuable than time.

There are many ways to start to appreciate your time more – and a starting place for me was the realisation that to make time support you, you have to respect it …

Your attitude and mental association with time is largely connected with your regard for this precious resource. Arriving late, leaving late, over-running a meeting, are all cardinal sins that will always come back to haunt you. I would even include arriving early for something and not being prepared by having something to do while you are waiting.

Often, if I have agreed to meet someone at a railway station for example, I will convert my car into a mini office and squeeze my value-for-money from the minutes that I am forced to spend waiting around.

Now, don't get me wrong, I am not obsessive over all of this. You won't catch me doing things like this on a weekend or on holiday, though I would want to do something enjoyable and/or useful with spare time. I never ever understand people who are waiting for someone or something, looking like a zombie into the distance as if they're in a hypnotic trance on the Paul McKenna Show.

Get in the habit of carrying non-urgent and non-important things you ideally need to spend time on in the back of your car or somewhere in your briefcase if you carry one. In our profession, there is a certain amount of reading we need to do if only to keep up to date with what's happening in our industry. This is prime carry-around material.

Using time to sell more effectively

Provided you always sell with a high degree of personal integrity, then whatever tools you chose to use, should be subtle rather than too obvious. You will be surprised how many professional people appear to not be selling when exactly the opposite is happening.

I am fairly convinced that if you spoke to any of my existing clients, and asked them how sales-orientated my meetings with them were – I would be staggered if they didn't look at you as if you were asking a ridiculous question. I make no secret of the fact that I do sell at every meeting, and am proud of the fact, yet my method of selling is always laid back and extremely subtle. In fact, the more subtle it is, the more sales I tend to make.

People do say sometimes that I can afford to be subtle, but you know, I never used to be when I first started – and I noticed how much of a struggle it sometimes was to 'close the business'. It was when a top producer remarked to me, *'You know, Sandro, I think if you relaxed a bit and stopped trying so hard, you'll find more sales come your way.'* As soon as I acted on his advice, I instantly noticed a difference and never looked back. One of the 'levers' I started to use in this process was around time.

Quite simply, I would always meet prospective clients at unusual times. If I wanted to meet someone at ten o'clock in the morning, I'd make it 0950 or 1010 – a slightly unusual time, for two reasons.

Firstly, people remember an unusual time, and because it is unusual, it strangely enough appears to have more value attached – because we associate it with professional services like doctors, dentists and lawyers.

Secondly, it indicates a busy person. It's people who are not that busy who use times like 1000, 1030 and 1100. Can you see how subtle this is? Also you must ensure you finish on time – albeit 1120 or 1135, which is written upon the agenda.

By the way, never be seen to be looking at your watch in a meeting. I will often surreptitiously look at the other person's watch to read the time or roll my sleeve up so my watch is visible and sneak a rapid glance when the person looks away. When I bring the meeting to a close, I invariably see the other person look at their watch and I can tell they are impressed when they realise there are only a couple of minutes to go.

One of the biggest mistakes people make around time control is sitting with a client 'for the duration' as a sign of good customer service. This is fraught with problems. It indicates a lack of respect for time and too much time on your hands which also says you are not that successful. I remember hearing of a story back in the eighties when hard nosed sales people would go to someone's home and sit

there refusing to move until they signed the application! In one case, the police were called as the last resort to remove the unprofessional sales person in question.

The green and red time exercise is interesting. Go back to a previous week in your diary. With green and red pencils, shade the areas of the diary with green for strategic time – important time spent, versus red time – wasted time spent. You need to do this properly. If you spent ten minutes doing nothing, shade it in as red. Lunch breaks are naturally shaded in green as you should have them, but if you eat lunch on your own and spend more than thirty minutes doing it … why?

Doing this exercise may shock you into realising how much time you waste each week. People often bleat, 'If I only had more time'. In all probability they do, it's just that they fail to respect the fact and adhere to a few simple time rules.

Planning and preparation

There's no doubt that good preparation is vital if we are to build firm foundations for a successful business. And if we are going to plan daily goals, then they must be inspirational and motivating in line with a time-aligned perspective. There's little point in creating a list of objectives if we do not have the time and therefore commitment or determination to make them happen.

In fact, it's better to have three objectives which you achieve one hundred percent, than five objectives and only achieve four.

Every time you make a commitment and fail to follow through, you are creating belief around your behaviour. You're saying it's okay to set a target and not achieve it.

Good 'Goal Getting' is about realism with some stretch attached. Achieve this and you're ready to do some more. This in turn makes you consistent and persistent.

Seven – Four – One

Most people are not aware that their brain switches off if they have too many things to do at one time. Psychologists have now declared it's between three and seven things. I Reckon that most of the female advisors I know would say say it's three for men and seven for women!

Seriously though, it's true. If you are in front of a client and have eight points to make, you inevitably start to lose their attention. Equally, making three points is probably more powerful than two.

Think about this when deciding on goals where time is a key component. We often waste time with too many things on our list of things to achieve. So the 7-4-1 system could be usefully deployed here.

- Identify **seven key areas** that are important to your success, e.g. prospecting, business administration, family, time off, networking and so on. You don't have to have all seven areas covered by the way.
- Once these areas are defined, then look at **four things that you need to achieve** in each area …
- … and the **one** of these four you've **highlighted to deal with next**.

How many of us struggle to tackle a problem or goal because it just seems beyond our capabilities to deal with it and with so many other 'plates we have spinning in the air'.

So, the best way of tackling goals like these is to break them down into smaller parts and handle each component part in a sequential order. The 7:4:1 approach is a simple idea which can be committed to a single sheet of paper and can be carried around in a diary

Tackling any goal – or indeed problem – in small manageable pieces will maintain enthusiasm and discipline levels – making it time-friendly too. After all, when was the last time you saw a world famous mountaineer attempt to conquer Everest without establishing holding camps at strategic points along the way? Top sports people do not take to the field without hours – and sometimes days – of practice on each and every different aspect of their game.

Stop managing your time

It is quite obvious that most people appear to have vastly more things to do than they have time to do them. Despite this, I'm not hugely keen on time management training. To me it completely misses the point. If you are trained how to manage time it also means you are

being made to manage tasks. However, who says you should be doing that task in the first place. Time management is a sophisticated way of saying … 'Plate Spinning System'.

Instead of managing your time, what about leading it? Being in control of it rather than it being in control of you.

Let me put it another way. If you knew today you had 22 hours left to live, would you manage your time to fit in all the things other people wanted you to do? Or would you crystallise and achieve exactly what you wanted to do in the little time you had left? I know one thing. You wouldn't spend eight hours going to sleep! Time leadership then is leading time in a way that supports your goals rather than manages them. The first principle is 'the why question'. *Why* would I want to do that? If there is a clear benefit, fair enough. If there is no benefit, remove it from your planning.

Here's an example – a new prospect rings you up and asks to do a small piece of business worth $60. You explain that you'd be delighted to help but learn they live 50km away. You ask them to come to you but they insist they want you to travel. You weigh it up and realise that this is a drain on your time and doesn't make any financial sense either. So you call a colleague nearer to the prospect and pass the business to her. That's time leadership and common sense.

Equally you're asked to attend a meeting. It will mean four hours of travel for one hour. You look into it and suggest you call in on a conference line when required. Of course, you may have to challenge people and convince them too, but do you want to lead or manage your business? Lead or manage your time?

Potential time stealers

It is all very well being aware of what makes time leadership effective but we also need to know what obstacles can get in the way so we can avoid or eliminate them. These things can cause 'displacement thinking' or 'interference' which are huge mental distracters.

☒ Overly lengthy discussions on phone – keep calls brief

☒ Drop-in visitors – arrange a proper time in your diary (if you want this!)

☒ My door is always open – close it.

☒ Drop-in visitors who won't go – you leave the office (go do something else more important, then come back)

☒ Excessive socialising – guzzles time like thirsty champagne drinkers and just as expensive.

☒ Other people rambling on in conversations – politely interrupt and summarise

☒ Members of your team making mistakes – are you coaching them?

☒ You losing control – no planning or MindChangers

☒ Doing too much reading – read when your are waiting for people, cooking, planes, trains, taxis, having a haircut …

☒ Indecision by you – get a mentor to help you

☒ Fear of small mistakes – learning and growing demands mistakes

☒ Postponing the unpleasant or difficult – it only gets more painful

☒ Doing other people's jobs for them – check your sanity

☒ Doing too much at the same time – 7-4-1

☒ Can't get jobs finished – reduce number you are doing and complete 100%

☒ Travelling – use this time strategically: hands free calling, reading if on train etc

☒ Phoning the same place or person several times when you could have done it in one or two calls – have calling times twice a day and limit call backs accordingly

☒ Spending a long time looking for paper or information – get a secretary who is organised.

- ☒ Paper shuffling in general – try and touch paper only once (this really works!)
- ☒ Doing valueless or pointless tasks – delegate or ditch task
- ☒ Forgetting to do/say things – have a good time organiser
- ☒ Doing tasks in an illogical or inefficient order – do the worst first as your time effectiveness maxim
- ☒ Not having the necessary information available.
- ☒ Lack of concentration or your mind wandering too much.
- ☒ Re-working tasks done inadequately first time round.
- ☒ Perfection in tasks where adequacy would do – happens all the time to inexperienced business people. Avoid!
- ☒ Always looking for mistakes – look what's working first

For those who would like to start thinking more about how to better control time, the score sheet overleaf will help you identify what may be some of the main problem areas. It continues to be a great track to run on for me personally.

Rank 4 (strongly agree) 1 (strongly disagree)
Be extreme – try to avoid using the middle ground if possible.

		4	3	2	1
1	I know exactly what my objectives are and those of my business.				
2	I can list the most important tasks I do daily				
3	When I start a new day, I always know what I need to do strategically.				
4	I usually do the important things FIRST rather than tasks that need to be done urgently.				
5	I usually plan how I organise my time.				
6	I always complete what I set out to achieve each day.				
7	I never spend longer on the phone than I should.				
8	Most of the meetings I attend are an excellent use of time.				
9	I usually set realistic deadlines.				
10	It is feasible to reduce the number of visitors I see/time I spend with them.				
11	I'm good at saying 'no' and avoid getting involved in everything.				
12	I believe that it is possible to control my time better.				
13	I give a reasonable amount of thought to how I do my job.				
14	The telephone saves me more time than it wastes.				
15	Rarely do I tend to bite off more than I can chew.				
16	When I do something, I don't spend too much unnecessary time 'finishing it off'.				
17	I always make sure that when I'm running meetings, they only last for as long as they were planned to or finish sooner.				
18	I tend to focus my time on the things that matter.				
19	I am good at making my own decisions.				
20	In my business, people usually complete their daily workload by 5.00 pm.				
	Totals				

Scoring: 0-39: You need to take action to improve. 40-59; Good but there are things you can still improve. 60-80; Excellent, but what else could you do to control your time more?

Whilst this score sheet will hopefully help identify some key issues, it does not provide answers. The key to mastering our time effectively does require us to embrace the belief that we're not helpless victims of the commercial world. Instead, we're all responsible for how we action our own time and prioritise things we have to do.

Daily planning questions

Most important when planning our working day is to ensure that we are free from distractions and interruptions, so here are some questions that I hope will help.

12 Questions to assist in preparing your daily action list:

- ? Of my long range high priority goals, which if any, should I work on today?
- ? What will help me get closer to these long range high priority goals today?
- ? Which projects will give me the highest return on my time investment?
- ? Is there a deadline to work to today?
- ? Which project will be the greatest threat to my personal survival if I don't do it?
- ? Which project will be the greatest threat to my company if I don't do it?
- ? What wasn't completed yesterday that needs to be done today?
- ? What does business suggest I should be doing?
- ? What does 'my gut' suggest I should be doing today?
- ? Is there anything else that may yield tangible results that I can do something towards today? (The 'stretch' element).
- ? What will happen if I don't do what I have to achieve today?
- ? What shall I award myself for 100% completion today?

How much is your time worth?

The following table calculates the actual hourly cost of time for people at various income levels. The value of each of your hours – even each of your minutes – is something to bear in mind when you review your diary record. Look at your time as money to invest. At your day-end summary, congratulate yourself for good 'investments' – and also pinpoint any that may not bear as high a yield.

Salary year	Salary week	Benefits = 40% total salary	Total week	Value per hour	Value per minute
5,000	96	38	135	3	0.06
6,000	115	46	162	4	0.07
7,000	135	54	188	5	0.08
8,000	154	62	215	5	0.09
9,000	173	69	242	6	0.10
10,000	192	77	269	7	0.11
15,000	288	115	404	10	0.17
20,000	385	154	538	13	0.22
25,000	481	192	673	17	0.28
30,000	577	231	808	20	0.34
35,000	673	269	942	24	0.39
40,000	769	308	1,077	27	0.45
45,000	865	346	1,212	30	0.50
50,000	962	385	1,346	34	0.56
55,000	1,058	423	1,481	37	0.62
60,000	1,154	462	1,615	40	0.67
65,000	1,250	500	1,750	44	0.73
70,000	1,346	538	1,885	47	0.79
75,000	1,442	577	2,019	50	0.84
80,000	1,538	615	2,154	54	0.90
85,000	1,635	654	2,288	57	0.95
90,000	1,731	692	2,423	61	1.01
95,000	1,827	731	2,558	64	1.07
100,000	1,923	769	2,692	67	1.12
125,000	2,404	962	3,365	84	1.40
150,000	2,885	1,154	4,038	101	1.68
175,000	3,365	1,346	4,712	118	1.96
200,000	3,846	1,538	5,385	135	2.24

Time tips I believe in …

These tips have helped me be more successful over the years and I heartily recommend them …

- ☑ Maintain a tidy desk.
- ☑ Be on time, start on time, finish early.
- ☑ Daily goals list.
- ☑ Delegate if possible.
- ☑ Say 'no' to jobs that aren't yours.
- ☑ Be assertive around time decisions.
- ☑ Set realistic deadlines yet don't make it too easy (where's the challenge in that?).
- ☑ Give yourself private time for a small part of the day.

Dealing with Interruptions

- ☑ Agree a time frame in a meeting and stick with it.
- ☑ Ask the person why they've come to see you.
- ☑ Stand up when they come in, and stay standing.
- ☑ Be ruthless with time, though gracious with people.
- ☑ Suggest you fix the meeting later.
- ☑ Make the meeting in the other person's office (so you can leave).
- ☑ Perch on the edge of the desk rather than sit down.
- ☑ Save small talk for the pub or bar.

The Golden Hour

One key time leadership technique that I used many years ago, and continue to use at least two or three times a week, is **The Golden Hour.**

Imagine setting aside an hour a day of quality time just for you. In this time you can decide what you want to do that would be most helpful to personal development. I have to say that, on occasions, I've used this to do things like catch up on correspondence with friends and create a birthday card schedule for the next twelve months. In other words, this hour is designed to allow you to have time to do those things that you often fail to do due to work pressures.

You could also have a golden business hour as well as a golden personal hour. The way the golden business hour works is that you get into the office very early when there are no telephone calls or other distractions and spend an hour of planning and preparation for the day/week ahead. The time should be entirely strategic and around important things rather than any-things!

The setting aside of a time slot and then putting into it important things relates to Parkinson's Time Law. This law tells us that unless we create tight, inflexible 'time compartments', we end up allowing what we do to spread through the day with no conceivable end point. In other words, if you set aside an hour to do a number of tasks, you will be more effective than doing it the other way round – ensuring you complete a number of tasks in however long it might take. So to utilise this time law effectively, it simply means creating a structure to any particular time slot with a specific deadline that you are aiming for and then doing as much as you can in that slot, knowing you have to stop at the deadline point. It's surprising how many people fail to do this when they are putting together a schedule for their daily routines when, by using this time control lever, they will find they become very much more effective.

To summarise, time is our most valuable resource which we can never repeat or save for a rainy day. We also can't acquire more of this resource from other people. The moral then is to ensure we plan and prepare sufficiently to be as effective as possible with our time control and do all we can to ensure time is not wasted needlessly. I like to think of it as a cheque book. With a money cheque book, we certainly don't like to write cheques unless they need to be written. Equally, if you had a time cheque book, would you be so generous in writing out these types of resource cheques? I doubt it.

End-of-chapter classic quotes

'Have the courage to tell people what you do, but never tell them how much you know. Learn to listen and find out how much they know.'

'Learn as much as you can about the products you represent, but always remember that a sale is 75% the art of listening and salesmanship and only 25% product knowledge.'

'Never be afraid to tell someone you don't know the answer to his or her question. They will appreciate openness much more than listening to you trying to bluff through a situation.'

'Have the courage to fail – that's how you gain experience.'

'Never, ever, give up. Remember that your next meeting could open up a world of possibilities.'

'Make friends with wise people.'

'Know your weaknesses. What you don't do well, have done by people who have strengths in those areas. Your biggest strength is knowing what you can do; not what you can't.'

ACTION STEPS

1. Score time management strengths and weaknesses regularly. Eliminate time stealers now.

2. Calculate how much your time is worth, if you don't already know. Commit to working only at a profit.

3. Use at least five of the time management ideas within your life and/or business.

4. Diarise and commit to at least one golden hour.

5. Categorise all your clients. Know exactly which ones are profitable and which are not – and invest your time accordingly.

5

The Route to Quality Business

There's no question that people who know my business and how I operate, associate my working practices with quality business. Given that I do a lot of investment business, sometimes for millions of pounds, it means I'm working with high quality individuals or businesses who place a lot of trust in me. Clearly this hasn't happened overnight and it would be most unusual for a brand new financial adviser to be able to break into this marketplace overnight. Although I believe that this is largely true, I do remember one point in time where I decided that my prospecting strategy had to change – and it did, overnight!.

This classic story is about the advisor visiting 'personal' or 'domestic' clients late in the evening at their home. Like many newly qualified financial advisers, I had mistakenly listened to some of the less successful advisers of the time who assured me that the route to success was working in the evening with couples and families. Whereas I see looking after this market as extremely important, it is definitely not a good idea to specialise in it if, at the same time, you wish to dramatically grow your business and multiply your turnover two- or threefold.

So I often think back to that evening, driving back in my car having spent three and a half hours of hard work, desperately trying to convince a married man with two young children he needed some life assurance. Eventually, after what seemed to be almost a pitched battle, he agreed to a meagre amount of cover which was better than nothing. Even so, I did wonder what benefit this was doing my own family who were at home waiting for my late arrival.

The next day, I decided that things had to change. I started to look at a new strategy and decided rather than spend 80% of my time in the domestic market and 20% of my time in the business market, to flip it over. I seriously began to look at the possibility of 80% of my time in the business and high net worth marketplace. Today this is much more like 90-95% of my time, and when I compare today with the days gone by, I'm currently much more successful, have less stress, have more time with my family, and I am ten times happier. You see for me, it was a choice I made that many financial advisers believe is not something in which is available to them.

So, right now, you are probably wondering what the magic formula is. How can you dramatically change your fortunes, and indeed your lifestyle, by making some minor mental alterations? First, I refer you to the chapter on MindChangers and suggest you use some of these basic tools as part of the process. Second, that you start to use some simple but highly effective techniques to beat a path out of the 'domestic jungle'.

In order to do this you will require a map. This chapter is about creating such a map and, once you have it in your hands, I will explain how to ensure you follow the right directions to arrive at your chosen destination.

Re-thinking the basics

Let's look at some of the methods that I strongly advise you to deploy in your new high net worth strategy.

1. Breaking into the corporate market

One of the reasons I set up Forte Global Consulting was to offer financial advisers around the world an instantly successful methodology that would help their businesses grow fast in what is still the largest untapped market for financial advisers the world over: the Corporate Market.

The workshops and personal coaching are based on creating a tool-kit of levers and techniques that work just about every time, in

any country, when dealing with business people and those who have a high level of personal wealth.

Although there isn't the space to expand on it all in this chapter, you may like to consider some foundation premises that will help you break into the corporate market.

(i) Perception of the financial adviser

The first reason businesses and high net worth individuals avoid talking to professional financial advisers and planners, is largely dictated by their perception of such individuals. Today, there is no question that a professional adviser, who has completed all his or her training and examinations, is in a much better position to give investment and business financial planning advice than a banker or a tax advisor. In fact, these advisors are the first to raise their hands and admit they are not investment specialists. Of course, banks do have specialist departments, but their products tend to be solely those that the bank wants to sell. As for tax advisors – they are often too busy dealing with returns and associated number crunching to offer any true business financial planning.

So just imagine a financial adviser coming along who is able to truly offer something new and original which would genuinely make a difference to growing the client's business and boosting the profit on the bottom line. If you are not in a position to attend any of our workshops or coaching sessions, may I strongly advise you to look into adding value to the services you are able to offer business and high net worth clients. With a few simple concepts that any self-respecting financial adviser could learn quickly, concepts that would help to reduce overheads and increase sales, suddenly you, the adviser, will be highly sought after to the extent that you will be invited to visit business owners, rather than having to rely on a hit-and-miss prospecting script..

The book I would highly recommend to any financial adviser who wants to get into the business marketplace, is *The E-Myth Revisited* by Michael Gerber. Being able to appreciate the contents of this book and then helping small to medium-sized businesses use some of the basic principles, would definitely give you a new form of respect in front of your prospects and clients.

(ii) Being able to read a balance sheet

Either by reading about it or getting a friendly accountant to explain it to you – being able to find your way around a balance sheet is of tremendous importance. I am often amazed how many financial advisers have absolutely no idea about business balance sheets and that's rather like saying you are a doctor yet haven't the first idea about first aid. Become familiar and comfortable with a business balance sheet and then request to see the same from your business prospects. Once more, there are a number of things that you could glean from looking at this financial document and it's highly likely you would be able to make some recommendations as part of this research process.

(iii) Charge a fee

I've always found people to be very predictable, particularly around getting things for free. The fact is people do not value the things they get for free. This is especially true in business and if you offer too much for nothing, then your client or prospective client simply ends up not taking you seriously. If you are going to deploy your business tool-kit for a particular client and it means working with them for a few hours every fortnight or month, then you must ask for a fee. If someone is paying for your advice – guess what, they'll end up taking it! By the way, have you thought of levying a small fee each time you sign up a new client? As strange as it may seem, the challenge in all of this is not the client, but in the mind of the adviser! If all your clients were paying a few pounds or dollars in subscriptions, they are unlikely to end up as someone else's client and are highly likely to do more business with you each and every year.

Of course you will need to create a value proposition so that the client is more than happy to pay the subscription, however there are so many things you can do for your client base that this is a relatively easy matter to resolve.

2. Networking

The old phrase goes – it's not what you know it's who you know. True or false? I have to admit that if I were to dispense with all my contacts, doing quality business would become much more difficult. However, networking and attracting quality business is not something which happens over a few days. This is very much a farmer with a sack of seeds, casting them into fertile earth that's been well prepared, and, over a period of time, seeing the seeds grow into plants, bushes or even oak trees. The reality is that anyone can sow the seeds, and provided the seeds are sown in the right way, a good crop is nearly always produced.

Over the years, I have been staggered by some of the people who have approached me in the same way. These are business people who are looking for me to introduce them to people I know. Yet it has only taken me a few moments to make up my mind because, as always, first impressions (and second impressions) still account for a lot. So the people who have approached me and had very short meetings with me are those who've appeared totally unprofessional in terms of their overall appearance, business dress, accoutrements (the things they carry or that are associated with them) and what they actually say in the meeting. In other words, is it a lot of hot air or am I convinced and impressed by their words?

I remember a successful financial adviser, back in the 1980s, who specialised in investments. Every year he would buy two first-class tickets on the QE2 cruise ship where he and his wife would go on a luxury (but working) cruise! They would see the large ticket price as a drop in the ocean compared with this fantastic opportunity to mix with the rich and famous. Think about this – a captive audience who they were interacting with for two or three weeks! However, their prospecting strategy was extremely subtle. People would wonder what business they were in, because they avoided telling them until it got to the stage where people were desperate to know what was it that made them so successful – after all, not everyone would be able to stay on such a luxury cruise ship. Only towards the end of the third week at sea would they relent and allow people to know they were in the investment business. Normally on the last day, lots of business cards and contact details would be thrust in their hands and their fellow passengers would ask them to promise they would contact them on returning to the UK. I think you get the overall idea here. Although this would be perhaps a little unprofessional today, the method behind it still stacks up. In other words, you have to invest to reap your rewards. If you don't invest in the right business clothes, accoutrements and some coaching/mentoring from those people who can put you on the right path, then you will fail to reach the right people you can become friends with, who will introduce you to quality prospective clients.

When I network with other professionals such as stockbrokers, bankers, attorneys and tax specialists, I will meet them at my health club or theirs, or at a restaurant. Although the conversation will be businesslike, it will not be too informal and I will ensure I give them a good impression in terms of what I say and how I say it. People are attracted to other people whom they respect and can trust. When was the last time you took a good hard look at yourself? Think about whether or not you could currently inspire other professionals to take you so seriously that they want to line up their clients to come and see you?

When I first joined the profession, I was very lucky to work with a man who was a fantastic networker, who could powerfully communicate his message in almost any situation. One of the things I well remember him sharing was an approach I later adopted with considerable success, along the lines of:

'I have no reason to expect that you would do business with me simply because we are friends, but I didn't think you would respect me if I didn't ask …'

He went on to say, *'Because of the nature of my business, I'd rather call you three years too soon than one day too late. Do you have any objections to getting together with me on a professional basis?'*

He further taught me that my prospects were all around me and that I shouldn't feel guilty of making presumptions about any of them. At times, when I would sit at my desk confronted with the chance of

a 'prospecting by phone' session, he would ask me, *'What's the worst thing that could happen if you make the next call?'* I would usually answer, *'They might say no.'*

He would see the apprehension on my face and calmly ask, *'What's the worst thing that could happen if you don't make that call?'*

It was then that I would really start to think. I would recall the commitment I made to myself and my clients when I first came into the profession. I would then pick up the phone and make the call with renewed inner strength. And, yes, there were the occasional rejections but the number of 'yeses' always compensated.

Another very effective way to ensure we make these important telephone calls is to put a note on or near the phone reminding us …

The thought of being rejected creates a fear which the best of us find challenging to manage. Yet taking action in spite of the fear is what separates the extraordinarily successful few from the below-average majority.

Isn't it great that we can actually decide which group we want to join!

3. Creating good publicity for your business

Many successful people in business have one other thing in common. They have some time and resources to devote to charitable events. The more successful I become, the more I seem to enjoy sharing this success with those who are perhaps not so fortunate.

For example, I currently work on the fund-raising committee of the National Society for the Prevention of Cruelty to Children's 'Caring for Children in Court' appeal. Through our efforts, we raise several million pounds for children who need emotional support during the process of securing a conviction against someone who has abused them in some way. Changing the lives of these young and vulnerable people is incredibly rewarding – but there are also the like-minded people you meet, mostly wealthy benefactors.

I have also chosen to reinvest some of the financial benefits I've been fortunate enough to enjoy from my business by becoming one of the biggest supporters of Million Dollar Round Table's Foundation. Again, two things – hugely fulfilling and exposure to loads of people who share similar goals.

The other side of all of this is that I get publicity, which tends to attract other business people's interest. And so I would heartily recommend that you think about different methods by which people can read or hear about you. These media methods include the local and financial papers, magazines, radio and television. One relatively easy route I would suggest is writing articles for trade and professional magazines. Although it is likely that these pieces will not in themselves earn you money, once they are published, you will attract readers who may be potential clients. They will also give you some material you can cut out and send to those who you would like to approach. Either way, the written word is always very powerful as people believe those things that are in print in bona fide newspapers and magazines. This is the way of the world – so use it to your advantage. Naturally, the article needs to be well written, with a good title, opening paragraph, something interesting the reader may learn and a good punchy summary. Remember to put contact details at the very end.

I recall a husband and wife team who approached a local London radio station some years ago, offering their services to listeners on a financial advice phone-in. To their surprise, the radio station was more than interested and they ended up doing phone-ins on a regular basis. Unsurprisingly, they subsequently had very many off-air conversations, and meetings that followed where a lot of investment and protection business was transacted.

I've done it myself, where I offered to support my local radio station with a summary of the Budget, a clear and concise appraisal of the government's announcements. It was amazing how I became something of a celebrity! Currently, I have a number of celebrity clients myself. Some of these people I approached completely cold,

and was successful because no other adviser had approached them before, and secondly I had really thought about the message I wished to give them which ultimately grabbed their attention and imagination. Believe me when I say that any financial adviser can do this if he or she has a mind to achieve it, and a serious passion to change their methods and overall strategy.

4. The personal introduction process

As a guest speaker at a number of events for financial advisers, I often hear other guest speakers talk about their methods and strategies for success. On the whole, I find listening to the words of wisdom from others fascinating and very uplifting. I hope they feel the same about what I have to say. However, there is a small percentage of guest speakers who leave me cold, because their suggestions are not only 'old hat' but totally unprofessional. The area that is most problematic is that around personal introductions. Here's something I've heard time and time again over the years that I'm sure is still suggested to financial advisers the world over. Personally I think it's dreadful.

Well Mr and Mrs Prospect, thank you for the business and I look forward to looking after you as your new financial adviser. At this point, I would like to ask you if you're entirely happy with the service I have provided so far? (Await their response.) Good, that's great. Tell me, do you have any friends or family who you think would also benefit from a similar discussion with me? (Await their response.) etc etc.

When I first joined the profession, I admit that I did exactly this as I was told it was the best approach. The results I got were very poor. Nowadays I would be highly embarrassed to do anything like this and would never recommend anyone using such a poor, unprofessional approach.

The reason why the above approach is unprofessional is because it comes out of nowhere. Your new client was not expecting to be asked for an introduction, and even if they were happy with the concept, you are putting them somewhat on the spot. When people are not expecting something, they tend to say words like, 'Oh, I cannot think of anyone,' or they will just give you a name at random to avoid the embarrassment caused by the question. Remember, you are not looking for just anyone – you want someone of their quality or more.

The personal introduction format

There are some really advanced ways to ask for personal introductions which we coach live or at our workshops. However, here is a general principle you may like to apply to your current method.

- ➔ At the beginning of the first meeting, introduce the fact you're going to ask for an introduction. Then mention it again towards the end of the first meeting, and actually ask outright at the end of the second meeting.
- ➔ Never ask for introductions from people who do not do business with you. The reason is that they are unlikely to endorse anything you do with the introductions they give, and they certainly would not give you quality introductions if they haven't got the faith and trust to do business with you in the first place.
- ➔ Always ask for a few introductions, not a long list.
- ➔ Make it a true personal introduction rather than some names and telephone numbers on a piece of paper. There is a massive difference.

So consider mentioning subtly at the beginning of the first meeting that you work in a professional way, mainly through personal introductions and then move on to something else. At the end of the same meeting, again you mention that much of your business comes from personal introductions and that existing clients have always been happy to recommend you in this way because of the high level of service you offer them.

At the second meeting, after you have possibly transacted some business, right at the end, mention it again. However, this time when you mention it you explain that unfortunately you are unable to accept more than two or three at a time. Nine times out of ten this will create

your first introductions from your new client and some will have already prepared this information in advance of the meeting! Now for some magic. When you receive the details, I strongly urge you to convert this information into a true introduction. Get your mobile phone out and ask your client to ring the person **now** so they may introduce you personally – live – while you are there.

Think about this. If it's a personal introduction, surely it should be done in a personal way. What could be more professional than your new client setting up the conversation and then passing the phone over to you? Remember, you do not wish the client to say too much as they may say the wrong thing – however if they are by your side throughout the entire conversation, it is a totally different approach and infinitely more successful than going back to the office with a strange phone number and name where you're almost starting from scratch.

I'm amazed that most advisers have never thought of doing this before. Yet surely this has to be the most effective way of getting personal introductions.

5. Friends and family

I remember, all those years ago when I first joined the profession, being told by a manager that it would be very easy to prospect because my friends and family would be able to give me lots of people to see. In reality, this is simply not true. My friends and family are like anyone else – they are very reluctant to offer introductions to people they know well as they do not wish to lose their friendship by involving them in something that they know little about – even though they may be a good friend or relative.

Yet the big benefit in dealing with friends and family is their close connection to you and, with the right process, they are normally willing to help if they can, and if they are comfortable with what you're asking.

The approach I recommend then is as follows:

☑ Make sure your friend or family member is your client first, and ensure he or she is highly impressed by what you've done.
☑ Make sure they clearly understand what the benefit would be to recommending you to people they know.
☑ Follow the personal introduction process as already outlined to the letter and avoid cutting corners with this group, even though you know them so well.

6. The talking business card

Though there are many more ideas I can list here – there is one more I would definitely like to share with you. Once more, this is an idea I've shared with many financial advisers, yet very few follow through and take action. The advisers who have done something about it have reaped the rewards many times over. As always, it's up to you.

If you can't rely on others to talk about you, you certainly can rely on yourself! Do this by writing a script about your business, your offering, what you can do for prospective clients. Take this script to a professional recording studio and make it into a polished CD or cassette. Have an elegant and professional label designed and printed. Now make a point of giving away a copy of this with your business card at every appropriate opportunity. In fact, this recording could be given away by your friends, family or even existing clients. When I first did this, I had no idea as to some of the wealthy and famous people it would lead me to. Such a simple idea – with minimal outlay – that could really work to your advantage. Just as a final point, ensure that the content makes what you do sound exciting, original and highly beneficial.

End-of-chapter quotes

'Anything will work if you do.'

'Work hard and stay in the game – even if it feels like you are not succeeding. Perseverance and hard work ensure success.'

'Learn to think big and find ways to associate with the people who are top in your industry – the people who are doing the things you want to do.'

'Choose a goal that is way out there – beyond anything you've ever done before. Consider carefully if you want to achieve it. Then, mentally, buy the ticket and go to work. You'll be amazed at how things come together.'

'Talk to everyone – often.'

'Most of my business came because I created networks. Soon you develop a wide reputation as the expert in this or that area but also as a solid, reliable, knowledgeable person.'

ACTION STEPS

1. Create a new perception within your client and contact list by really considering what you do that is different.

2. Commit to spending more time networking than any other activity.

3. Work on, and start using, a new personal introduction which is more effective than the one you are using currently.

4. Use, as often as possible, the personal introduction 'script'.

5. Visit your top twenty clients. Ask them to help in building your business through quality personal introductions – help them to network in return.

6. Start now – never make a promise that you know you cannot keep.

6

The Amazing Client Offering

It all started many years ago when I caught up with an American friend over a drink and he told me about his recent visit to New York. He explained that he met one of the top New York financial advisers of the time, located on Wall Street. He described their well-appointed offices and how impressed he was with the valet parking on arrival and the well- planned office layout, together with the high quality fixtures, fittings and furniture.

He went on to describe the warm positive reception he received and the fact that his name was up in lights on a welcome board.

He was shown into a sumptuous reception room complete with an imposing chesterfield and an array of quality magazines that could only be described as dramatic. On top of this he was offered a menu which included all sorts of beverages from various parts of the world. It even offered champagne with strawberries in season! There was the rich aroma of coffee drifting through from a side room, laced with the tantalising smell of freshly baked bread rolls. With pleasant uplifting music in the background, his senses were intoxicated, giving him an outstanding first impression of this business. Though he listed many more visitor-focused benefits, the two that really stuck in my mind were the fact that when he left he realised that his car had been completely valeted and when he returned for a follow-up meeting there was a different menu that day and the person who greeted him (someone completely different) knew his previous beverage order from the last visit. The word that sprung to mind was 'wow!'

When I thought about the level of this client offering, it occurred to me that it made perfect business sense. Imagine how many clients

or visitors would make sure they come early to meetings in order to enjoy some of this splendid hospitality. The other thing was that a lot of the ideas were small concepts rather than something completely incredible. Once again, another old adage – 'It's the little things that make the big difference…'

So now I have a challenge for you. Get a piece of paper and a pen, draw a line down the centre of the page and in the left-hand column make a list of everything you currently do for your clients/customers that would impress them enough to talk about it to other people. I really do mean this – if you're already reading on, please stop. Find some paper and a pencil and do this exercise as I know it will be very valuable to you.

So how did you get on? Okay, now make a list in the right-hand column and write down every idea which you believe is entirely original – in other words, not being practised by anyone local who may be perceived as a competitor.

Difficult isn't it!

For me it's always difficult to offer a level of service that no one else in the world is offering. When you think of the same concept countrywide it becomes a little easier, and when you relate it to your county or state, in other words locally, it becomes easier still. What isn't acceptable, may I suggest, is doing things the same way that everyone else does in your business. Where is the point to this? By differentiating yourself – or should I say *seriously differentiating* yourself – you instantly have an opportunity of adding immediate profit to your bottom line.

Another story I remember hearing from the 1980s was of the financial adviser who had the habit of giving all his clients a leather wallet for their insurance and other financial documentation. It was a kind of 'thank you for doing business with me'. However, he made it clear that his leather wallet was on loan only for as long as they remained a client.

One day one of his clients rang up to say he had got a cheaper quotation for his term assurance plan and was cancelling his current policy. Believe it or not, the thing that really changed his mind about *not* cancelling was the adviser's retort: 'I understand, but could I ask

if you would kindly have your leather document wallet available for collection.' This little thing had made such a big difference to the way he perceived his plans. He'd rather stay a client and keep the leather wallet than return it and simply have some new paperwork in its place!

The fact is as consumers we make judgements about the suppliers of goods based on some rather illogical associations. It might be about the location, the way you are treated when you deal with the business, the business's telephone etiquette, the little additional extras and added value you get from doing business with that company and so on.

What you might wish to consider is having a brainstorm session with some or all of the members of your business and collectively creating then committing to providing some extraordinary client care that makes those clients talk about you to their friends, family and colleagues.

One really exceptional way to find out what your clients/customers really want is to put together a Client Focus Group and essentially entertain a number of your clients at the end of a business day, at lunchtime or maybe even on a Saturday morning. Offer full hospitality with a couple of brief presentations so they can go away with some information about growing their wealth for example, things they would find really invaluable. Make sure they all realise that the primary objective of the hospitality is to find out as much as possible from them in terms of their current experiences with your business and what you think would make your business even better in terms of customer service.

Some time ago, I attended one of these sessions with my local accountant. Apart from enjoying the hospitality which had been well prepared, it was good to offer feedback and air frustrations and irritations that I now felt someone was taking seriously. It also made me realise that the firm were serious about looking after their clients – otherwise why would they go to such expense and trouble?

I can imagine that the reason more businesses fail to take this approach is their resistance to investing in their business like this, not to mention their worries about receiving negative feedback. However,

if you fail to find out what isn't working, it can never get better (in fact, it only gets worse) and will undoubtedly impact your profitability in the long term.

If I was to make a list of the key areas that need attention in respect of good customer care, they would be as follows:

- e-mails
- surface mail
- over the telephone (inbound and outbound calls)
- ad hoc mailings and advertising
- front-of-house reception
- speed in answering queries, either by letter, e-mail or telephone
- a damage limitation customer plan – in other words what action to take if a mistake has been made or a customer has a less-than-satisfactory service experience.

I have to say I have been completely and utterly amazed by some well-known businesses on the last point. Where mistakes have been made and the business's reputation is on the line, the things I have been offered have been, dare I say, positively insulting. The worse example I can cite is turning up for a pre-paid flight at the airline counter only to be told that the flight had been overbooked, then being provided with a voucher for a drink and a sandwich along with a six-hour wait and a curt apology. Outraged, I have never travelled with that airline ever again.

From my side, I remember travelling to meet a client and unfortunately getting stuck behind a motorway pile-up. Though there was not a lot I could do, I knew it was unforgivable to arrive forty minutes late. Though my client seemed understanding, after the meeting I rang the local florist and ordered a large bunch of flowers for the reception desk in her office. To this day, she still mentions this fact – astonished at a gesture which cost me a few moments on the telephone and a few pounds on my credit card. However, she has continued to send me introductions to the extent that those flowers have been paid for hundreds of times over.

Another aspect that has stood me in good stead with my clients is knowing as much about them as possible. Whenever I meet a client, I scribble notes of any new information they give me, particularly personal details. This seemingly irrelevant information pays big dividends, given that I review this material before meeting with the client the next time. Knowing little bits of information about them, their friends, their pets, their family and children and recalling this really differentiates me as someone they respect and rely on. Put another way, I am seen as someone who cares, rather than just as a person with whom they do business – I hope more like a friend. Even though all this information is written down, people assume that you simply remembered it and this always pays your customer such a high compliment. How much personal information do you know about your clients? Have you ever been interested enough to find out such knowledge and record it in their file notes. Like all the ideas in this book, the tools and techniques are easy to implement. However, they do require a small amount of commitment towards *daring to be different*.

The big area of differentiation

Earlier, I listed some of the ways you can really differentiate yourself. One of these was around the use of a telephone. It's my firm belief that the way your telephone is answered and the way people are spoken to underlines the quality and calibre of your business. It's your shop window – the one your customers look into and get a real sense of who they are dealing with.

Once more, I am amazed by some of the largest organisations in the world who appear to be completely oblivious to the standards they apparently endorse around the use of the telephone in their business. Employees appear poorly trained, have little understanding of the importance of rapport and alignment with callers, and in some cases appear to be begging for a fight! It's quite staggering. Sometimes you are spoken to in an overtly patronising way when you know the person doesn't mean what he or she is actually saying. The classic is,

'How may I help you?' followed by a 'couldn't-care-less' attitude.

If you run your own business, you may like to get some mystery callers to ring in and test how good your team are. Be careful here as it would not be a good idea to do this in such a way that you undermine your colleagues. However, it can give you an inkling of how good your telephone 'system' is in relation to caller perception and satisfaction.

Things to avoid over the telephone

- not sounding genuine to callers
- appearing unhelpful
- using terms like 'is in a meeting' and 'I have no idea where she is' etc
- giving callers the 'third degree'
- failing to match the tone, volume and speed of your caller
- failing to return calls promptly
- failing to listen carefully to what the caller is saying, and jumping to conclusions too early in the conversation
- ringing off before the caller does.

A really good investment for your business would be to get someone in who can coach your team in good telephone etiquette and call handling. It really does pay immense dividends in the short, medium and long term. And if it's done well by an organisation who know what they are doing, you'll get terrific feedback almost immediately from customers and contacts who call in.

A final telephone tip concerns the number of rings before a phone is answered. If you can get this right, it's definitely a huge differentiator as many businesses completely ignore any standard around how long they keep their customers waiting. The ideal number of rings is two or three – four is probably too many and one too few. Of course, no customer is going to complain if the phone is answered after a single ring, though some customers find it a little unnerving if there are no rings at all. Once it gets to four rings and beyond, then there is the danger of customers believing that you do not value their

business. Often they are right! As a customer yourself, don't you find it very frustrating to be hanging on the end of a telephone, ring after ring? I suggest that if you do answer the phone after four rings, you apologise immediately as part of the telephone answering procedure. This can go some way to persuading the customer that it's not standard practice to keep them waiting for so long.

Final amazing thought

In recent times, I have travelled extensively around the Far East delivering presentations and coaching. I have found the service I receive in countries like China, Japan, Malaysia, Vietnam, The Philippines, Singapore and Taiwan truly inspirational. The most amazing experience for me was when I was sitting drinking a cup of coffee in a well-appointed hotel. I was suffering from a mild headache and remembered I had some aspirin in my pocket. So I took out a couple of tablets and put them on the side of my saucer thinking how nice it would be to take them with some water. Suddenly I looked up and saw the smiling face of a waiter who presented me with exactly that – a glass of freshly poured iced water! Naively, I thought 'what a coincidence, I was just thinking of that.' Then of course, I realised he had spotted me take out the aspirin and decided to do something utterly astonishing: he read my mind! That is what I call an amazing customer offering.

End-of-chapter quotes

'Learn to think big and find ways to associate with the people who are at the top – the people who are doing the things you want to do.'

'Life is what happens to you when you are busy making plans.'

'Men are convinced by reasons they themselves discover.'

'Value must always exceed cost.'

'In the middle of difficulty lies opportunity.'

'To make progress, we must be strong enough to be weak.'

'The results we get in life are based on our approach to life.'

'Star performers know the difference between success and significance.'

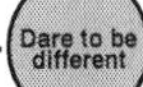

ACTION STEPS

1. **Create a minimum service standard for your business. Write it down, share it with everyone you meet – and stick to it like glue!**

2. **Organise a client appreciation event. Share the cost with others if you must, but let your clients know that you care.**

3. **Practice sharpening your conversational skills. Try starting a conversation in an elevator, during a seminar or some other public event.**

4. **Create a list of six prospective professional introducers. Call them to ask for a meeting to discuss ways you might help one another grow your respective businesses – maybe by introducing clients.**

7

Creating a Professional 'Feeding Lane'

To start with, it is probably worth clarifying what I mean by 'the Feeding Lane'. This is best explained by highlighting the behaviour of salmon – fish that, rather unusually, swim upstream in order to feed.

Of more significance however, is the fact that salmon will only attempt to eat what appears directly in front of them for no other reason other than their vision is extremely limited. Yet what this creates as a useful advantage by accident, is an extraordinary level of tunnel vision and focus.

The learning from this analogy is simple. Imagine being the same way when we want to improve the quality of our business, indeed our lives.

If we focus on the things that make us as productive as possible whilst not wasting huge amounts of energy in the process and aim this towards a positive outcome, we start to do what most financial advisers are simply not doing all over the world – thinking the 'less is more' principle.

There's nothing more liberating than meeting up with a prospective client for a coffee or lunch, agreeing a way of working together, discovering a mutual love of playing golf, meeting at the local golf club the next time, completing the paperwork for the business near the eighteenth then playing a round of golf to cement the new working relationship.

There are two essential elements to highlight in this example, apart

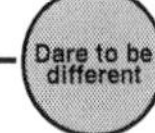

from being able to play golf in the first place! Seriously, you first need a *professional introduction* to make this more of an uncomplicated process and secondly you have to have a passion to maintain the momentum. Very little ever happens by pure chance. It is about focusing on what you want and having the courage to keep going, even when everyone around you – most of them failures in life – tell you 'it can't be done.'

When I do focus on the outcome, as I do with all my high net worth clients, I can identify the specific processes I planned, then implemented, to get the outcome. You must do the same. To come home after an enjoyable day's golf (or whatever you are interested in doing more of), having made money doing it – is the most invigorating and inspirational feeling. I contrast this with my early days in financial services, spending all day seeing as many clients as possible, knowing that only a few would want to be my client at the end of the day. All that activity and a disproportionately small return for the investment of my time.

The world's most successful financial advisers – those I regularly meet at MDRT for example – have built their businesses by either establishing a reputation as an expert in a particular field (and receiving numerous introductions as a result), or else creating lasting relationships with existing clients or other professionals.

By the way, the idea of being a specialist is very important. People like specialists rather than generalists. You know what they say about 'Jack of all trades' don't you… Being a specialist gives you an edge over the competition and a 'handle' to hang your professional coat on.

There is certainly no shortage of opportunity to create a 'feeding lane' in most countries. In the UK alone, there are currently 15,000 professional firms, both legal and accountancy practices, offering financial advice 'in-house'. But with the ever-changing face of legislation and regulation, this is expected to drop to a mere 2,000.

Clearly these firms do not want to be in a situation where they have to say to clients, 'sorry, but we can't deal with you any longer', so this in turn represents an unprecedented opportunity for us to broaden our horizons and develop new business relationships.

Attorneys, lawyers and tax advisors (CPAs) have a duty of care to their clients which is why they should be looking to approach other businesses which could assist with the all-round service they have provided in the past. The key to that relationship is to provide such high quality levels of service to the introducers – who always remains accountable to their clients – that your deliverables reflect on their own business, putting them in a good light.

The task is made much easier if we establish a niche. The specialisation could just be a concept or something simple like a particular Unique Selling Proposition. Once it has been established that your business is unique, there is a much better chance you will be sought after by both existing clients and professional centres of influence.

There are several examples of this type of business positioning:

- ☑ lowest price/lowest quality
- ☑ highest price/best quality
- ☑ best service
- ☑ friendliest service
- ☑ widest choice
- ☑ most convenient.

Competing on price is going to lead to problems because there will always be someone willing or able to offer cheaper products and services. There will always be a competitor with lower overheads, better technology – or perhaps be prepared to sell at a loss in order to gain market share.

Some clients are willing to have only the best – and are therefore willing to pay for the best. This is why prestige vehicle manufactures continue to sell motor cars and why Rolex and Cartier are still in business. By the way, if you buy a gold Rolex, it's not because you want to tell the time!

General financial planning can provide a wide degree of choice, although whatever is offered should be relevant to the particular marketplace. Sometimes too much choice causes confusion so it might be the most convenient service which appeals – for example those who wish to purchase from the internet. And it costs absolutely

nothing to provide a friendly service, although care should be taken to ensure that our clients' perception of the manner in which we run our businesses matches our own.

There is certainly no suggestion that any of the above constitutes anything less than a sound business model. To succeed, everyone must have quality underpinning the business model, because that is what most prospective clients and customers are seeking. Sometimes (rather unfortunately) it is because they have had a bad experience elsewhere.

Building professional relationships is a process based on universal principles that must be learned, believed and applied. If you think about the relationships most valuable to you, you will probably find that they are based on shared values. If you can identify this as being the case, then you have a great opportunity to spend some time considering almost endless possibilities. Healthy professional relationships are based on mutual respect for the knowledge and expertise both parties bring; so taking the time to study, plan and incorporate some sound business principles will certainly not do you any harm. We all need to be aware that the more we give in terms of respect, the more respect we gain. The more we invest in life and business the more we get back.

It is difficult to overestimate the real benefits of selling, developing and implementing a long-term financial plan when creating a relationship with a client. But the result is compounded when we are able to successfully integrate the use of other specialists – professionals such as a tax adviser or attorney. This is either because we are looking to provide continuity, encourage long-term relationship-building or provide a quality, all-round, service for less. Whilst we may not be able to directly offer all the services a client may ever need, we should be able to call on our business 'partners' who can assist in building a 'One-Stop Shop' to customer loyalty. In effect this means that, with the several calls from your client each year to discuss the various things you manage (or co-ordinate) on his or her behalf, without actually providing anything other than you own specialism, you are offering a very effective and cost-efficient service.

Identifying the Right Strategic Partners

In originally setting up the Feeding Lane for my business, I was very naive to think that just by visiting accountants and lawyers, they would be delighted to introduce me to their clients. My thinking was clouded by the fact that I was convinced my ideas were so good that every professional would want to work with me. Unfortunately, it's not as easy as this, as I am sure you are aware.

Firstly, you can be the best financial adviser in the world, but if you can't answer the question, 'what's in it for them?', then you are lost. Of course there is kudos – your service in some way reflecting how good their service is – but it has to be greater than that.

Before you meet your prospective professional introducer, be very clear what your offering is, and what in turn you are offering them. Make it original and highly tantalising, majoring on what is different about you. For some, this is sometimes easier said than done.

Often in a group coaching session, or on consultancy work for Forte Global Solutions, I ask the business owner, *'So, what's different about your business?'* The responses I receive are often very underwhelming. Comments like, *'We like to give good service'*, and *'We care about our clients – and tell them so.'* My usual response is, *'Great! That's the same as just about every other self-respecting business like yours on the planet, isn't it?'*

Similarly, when you meet professional introducers, you have to have an 'edge' that they may use when they sell you to their clients.

I also find it compelling talking about how I could introduce business to them. Between twenty and thirty protection sales a week came my way after I approached a mortgage broker asking them if they wanted a streamlined process to help increase their revenue by 2-30%. Their eyes lit up. Normally in days gone by financial advisers would only be talking about one-way traffic introductions and how the spoils of the commission made would be divided.

So where do you start when looking for introducer prospects?

The best place might be to call up professional advisers you already know, but then go one step further and enquire how many other businesses like theirs they know. With a personal introduction from a fellow professional, there should be no real challenges in

arranging a meeting to see them.

When I started my own business, I set out to ensure that all my clients, almost without exception, would come by personal recommendation through either existing clients or professional advisers. I recognised early on that calling numbers from the telephone directory is hard work – and why work hard when it's so easy to work effectively.

To give myself a competitive advantage, I developed an Introducer Pack – a simple presentation document which comprised four sections.

The first was a **fax enquiry sheet**, which demonstrated to the potential introducer that I operated a system designed to ensure follow-ups and accurate record keeping. Most of all, the fax enquiry sheet was designed to illustrate a system that was 'slick' and professional. Both adviser and introducer would have a copy of the client introduction, so there would never be any lack of communication. Compare this with what most accountants and lawyers/attorneys have been used to in the past (a haphazard system of introduction, which is usually soon exposed as an unreliable and unprofessional arrangement), and I instantly got their attention.

The second section is simply a selection of **the standard letters** I use in the business process – from the introduction or welcome letter through examples of the communications we send to confirm the client meeting, a typical recommendation letter and other follow-ups we would send out as part of the client care (sales)process.

Section three is an example of a **weekly or monthly update** which usually details the name of the client with a brief paragraph summarising where we are in terms of the client sales process at any particular time.

This section adds a further dimension to the professional standards we're looking to set, demonstrating a willingness to provide regular feedback.

Section four provides an example of a **commission schedule,** assuming of course, we're looking to share commissions or fees with the introducer. This is the part of the Introducer's Pack which acts as the commercial 'hook' most professional firms will see as attractive.

However, some countries do not allow fee or commission rebates to introducers, and many advisers see it as unprofessional. Whatever your view, just be transparent about what you earn – it matters for a relationship based on trust and integrity.

The next stage to consider is calling a tax adviser (CPA) in your area explaining that you're looking for someone to whom you can refer a number of your business clients – the ones who regularly ask for quality tax advice. Imagine asking whether they would be interested in a brief discussion in respect of your introducing your clients to their business practice? How likely are they to say – 'Sorry, not interested'?

Given that it's likely the answer is 'yes' you now have an opportunity to establish at this first meeting whether the prospective introducer has any established relationships with other advisers; relationships which might compromise an association with your own business.

If there is no relationship or one in which the prospective introducer isn't completely happy with, then take the opportunity to demonstrate the unique benefits associated with a strategic relationship between the two businesses starting with a brief look at the Introducer Pack.

In my experience, it was simply a question of presenting a unique and genuine approach to the potential business relationship and, after that, the rest is easy.

However, the most important advice of all – *take action.* These guys aren't going to come to you until you have a strong brand and reputation. So follow the steps as outlined above and **be consistent and persistent.**

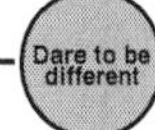

The Marketing Engine

Another way to create a cost-effective and constant stream of new business introductions is by creating a Marketing Engine.

Although there's no better place to start than with other professionals – existing clients can also be amongst the most reliable of advocates. Creating an environment where prospective clients can meet in what some people refer to as 'favourable circumstances' may be done through client seminars.

This needn't necessarily be a 'turn up and sit down' presentation to hand-picked clients. It might take the form of a social event with a brief informal opening at the start, then perhaps a short presentation before lunch/dinner so that people start talking enthusiastically about networking. The presentation has to match audience expectations – that the event will *dramatically enhance their business or life* depending on who is invited. It has to be so good they will want to come back time and time again.

Events like this can be very cost-effective, especially when compared with the huge amounts of money spent on buying lists of 'names' and then spending hours and hours cold-calling. So find twenty of your best clients or a few strategic business partners and prospecting the hard way will become a thing of the past.

So what is a marketing engine exactly?

Consider an old-fashioned engine with 4 to 6 pistons. Each piston drives the engine – or in this case – your business. Now name each piston as a resource for your introductions. Piston 1, for example, could be a tax adviser, piston 2 a lawyer, pistons 3 and 4 are existing clients who regularly introduce you through their business, piston 5 is networking through such as a Business Breakfast Club and piston 6 are leads from 'guesting' at events, local radio phone-ins or via a column in your local paper.

To create your engine you need a minimum of four channels of introductions and a maximum of six. Each 'piston' is structured and developed to provide the prospects, like a running tap that never gets turned off, and indeed prompts you to start thinking of a 'waiting list' for new clients desperate to get your advice and extraordinary service.

End-of-chapter classic quotes

'Everyone wants to be right but no one stops to consider if their idea of right is right.'

'You can't do something you don't know if you keep on doing what you do know.'

'To improve as a golfer – and as a person – you have to rise and fall alone and to learn exactly why it is you have risen or fallen'

'I tell my kids what my mum told me.
Everyone has to have a plan and for every plan you have, you need three more to back up the plan.
I planned things even as a kid.'

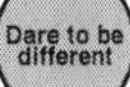

ACTION STEPS

1. **Use the following 'marketing engine monthly plan' template to create a 'to do' list of the opportunities you can create for yourself right now.**

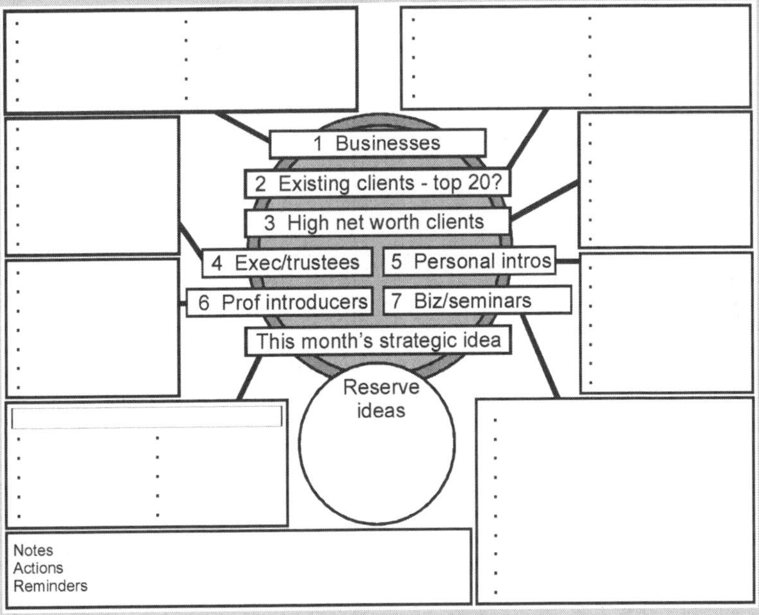

(Redraw this form yourself or photocopy and enlarge it)

2. **In order to make sure sufficient time is put aside in your diary to make the necessary calls each day, use the A-E diary system. Each day is divided into three sections, morning, afternoon and evening. Allocate a letter to each section according to the following suggestion: A = sales; B = background work (preparation); C = day off; D = hotel day; E = 'anything goes' day. Ensure that in any 30-day period, there are at least four D days.**

8

Putting your Mental Toughness to Work

Some time ago, I started to read about the whole subject of mental toughness – the type of thinking used by sports people the world over in their daily routines in order to ensure they have the best chance of winning in their chosen event.

This is no different to financial advisers wanting to be very successful in their own businesses, yet most would admit that they know very little about mental toughness. In this chapter, we are going to explore this important concept and its practical application.

I must warn you that your business – and life – may never be the same again. But, to make the difference, it will require those two crucial factors **consistency and persistence**.

I first heard about MindChangers from Glen McCoy in the early 1990s. Glen is a business performance coach who pioneered the link between the winning mind through sports psychology, and the winning mind in business performance.

A MindChanger is a mental toughness technique that is used on a daily basis, or once a week for techniques like the Image Diary. The idea is that any action or thought recreated for a minimum period of 28 days – the length of time it takes for any mental programming to take full effect – will become a habit.

An extraordinary thing I come across each time I meet financial advisers who are having a hard time is the admission that they do nothing about their core beliefs – the major reason for their drop in business success. Both attitude and behaviour are underpinned by

beliefs, so if you believe something that doesn't support your ultimate goals, you will not progress.

Imagine a top tennis player thinking she or he is going to lose miserably. It's a self-fulfilling prophecy I'm afraid, which is why sports psychology is so way ahead in its concepts and 'technologies'.

One major player in this game is Timothy Gallwey, the author of *The Inner Game*. What's abundantly clear to me, is whether you are a tennis player, swimmer, footballer, athlete, accountant, singer or financial adviser – the inner game is played each day, every day without any let-up. As you read and digest the pages of this book you're very much playing this game.

Ultimately people who can win at their very own 'inner game', the game they play in their mind at a subconscious level, are in a position to win at just about anything they choose to put their hand to. So much of anyone's success depends on mindset.

Some humans have it naturally and are mind-success naturals. Others, the vast majority, have to do a 'reset' or reprogramming job on themselves. However, everyone without exception has all they need to make their goals, ambitions, targets and dreams a reality. The only question is – how much do you really want it?

Consider the three basic truths about success.

1 If it was that easy, everyone would be a runaway success – how boring and uninspiring would that be?

2 True success is not about chasing money. It's about chasing dreams that manifest themselves as achievements which can be small to start, and build with time. As this happens, you tend to notice that money starts to chase you.

3 The best success comes as a result of genuinely helping others to be, say, healthier, happier or more wealthy – in other words, creating a better place for them as a result of your contribution. Crack this and notice how quickly you also benefit.

A moment's digression – I remember hearing about the time before legislation and the Financial Services Act of 1986, in the UK – a time where selling financial products was a 'free-for-all', a time when you could sell anything to anyone whether it benefited them or not. You could sell a new product to your unsuspecting customer each year and make a huge commission doing it. And many advisers did. The question is: where are all those advisers and what good did it do them? I know for a fact that just about every adviser who lacked integrity left the business. Here's the point – if you want to be successful, *always treat your clients the way you'd like to be treated.* It's the oldest sales advice in the world, yet consistently ignored time and time again.

Let's get back to creating mental toughness with MindChangers.

Mental toughness is knowing what must be done despite all the interference and mental barriers. I have benefited by mental toughness when I've run the Marathon. If you've ever done anything so punishing, you'll know why mental toughness is so important. Without it, I would never have completed my last Marathon – because one's body is at odds with one's mind. The body says, 'I've had enough', whilst your mind says, 'I can't stop now'. And this is where MindChangers make all the difference.

If you've programmed your mind for success, it simply re-runs the process when you most need it – and more often than not it carries you through like riding a high wave on a surf board. It's a wonderful feeling!

Just about every MindChanger technique is easy to perform, and you need only do two to three a day (more if you want of course), because two to three will get you a long way on your success journey. Let's look at some of these powerful mind tools. As we go through each one, put a mental tick against it and decide if it appeals to you.

At the end of this chapter I'm going to challenge you to select at least two and hopefully three of these techniques to use *consistently and persistently* until you make all your most important goals in life a stark reality. Are you game?

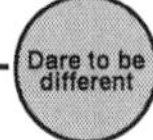

The MindChanger techniques in detail

The Walking MindChanger

It's interesting how much legwork we do each and every day. We walk out of the house, often to the car or local transport station. We walk to our offices or to see a client, walk to our desks, walk out of the office to get some lunch and so on. In all of these journeys we are often doing very little in terms of strategic outcomes. Of course, some of us are thinking about business matters, yet very often we are just wasting time with random thoughts.

Here's where the Walking MindChanger comes into its own. The idea is that, as you are walking from one place to the next – and this can be done on even the shortest of journeys – you set up a sentence in your head that you repeat in tempo with your walking pace. If you are walking slowly, then the sentence tempo will match the speed you are travelling. Does it his make sense? Let's imagine that the sentence is:

Isn't it amazing where this massive amount of business has come from.

Although some people have said this is rather like a 'mantra', I have to say it is very powerful and *does work*. What you are doing is programming this sentence and all the power and value it holds, driving it deep into your subconscious mind.

The essence of any MindChanger is to open a window in your mind which is currently closed and shuttered. By opening this window, you see opportunities that you would normally be oblivious to. Naturally, you can change your sentence – though I advise you to do this only after you've actually achieved the result you're looking for.

What you should choose for your first walking MindChanger is something really important to you – something that would have a great impact on your career, business or life as a whole. In fact, choose the subject matter now. Stop and think for a moment what would make the most difference to you. Is it having more meetings in your diary? More high net worth clients? Increasing your turnover? Getting more recommendations? Spending more time with your

family? Being better at a particular sport?

Having decided, create a sentence around it. When you write this sentence down, make sure it is in the past tense rather than a future wish or desire. In other words, what you write must have already happened, not something you hope will happen. This is important as most MindChangers are based on this concept. It is not an affirmation. An affirmation is something you are stating in the hope it will happen. A MindChanger is acknowledging that the wish or desire has already happened, even though in reality it may not yet have come to fruition. By actually phrasing things in the past tense – or in the worst case', the present tense – you are challenging your mind in terms of its credibility. When you believe something is true even though it's not, your subconscious rushes to make adjustments so that what it believes as being real and tangible manifests itself as reality. This is why a lot of people never ever see their dreams become reality. They keep wishing for something, and let's be fair, the majority of people on our planet are continually wishing for things that they never ever attain. Hoping for something is a weakness. Knowing you are going to make something happen – and then for it to happen – is extremely powerful.

You may like to record your Walking MindChanger somewhere that you can see regularly – in your time management system, on your bathroom mirror, on the door of the fridge, as a screensaver on your laptop…

I often associate MindChangers with the behaviour of children. Isn't it true how many children get exactly what they want by continually asking for it in different ways, never letting up until they get exactly what they want. Unfortunately, as adults we have forgotten that this works – and though you may not be addressing someone specifically, asking must happen before any type of receiving takes place.

The Coloured Dot

In any stationers, you can buy stick-on dots of different colours. Choose a set of your favourite colour, as this is going to be the basis of the next MindChanger that I suggest you decide to use.

This technique is based on imaging a strong picture of something

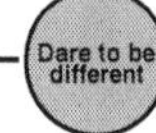

material and once a day looking at the coloured dot to make the picture in your head. See this dot grow in front of your eyes like a big circular TV screen and then look at the thing that you want to materialise. When I've used this type of technique, I've often seen large investment cheques that clients are offering me or I see a fully scheduled diary packed with people to see of high quality. You should spend two to three minutes making these images and associating them with your coloured dot.

Now take some dots and place them on things around you – your diary, calculator, DVD player and so on. Every time you catch sight of the dot, you will also get a quick burst of the energy and vision needed to help you towards your target – a great way to open windows in your mind.

A quick note: ultimately you will need to choose two to three MindChangers although you can engage in using all of them if you wish. It's a bit like going into a gym for the first time – do you want to choose a couple of pieces of equipment to get going or do you want to go on all of them? The choice is yours and I would personally select at least three MindChangers to use daily for the next 28 days.

The Lift

The Lift MindChanger is a non-material technique which is probably the most powerful of all MindChangers. This technique has been used in different guises by sports people over the last fifty to sixty years. It should be done on your own in quiet surroundings where you will be undisturbed. Having said this, I sometimes use this technique while sitting in my car waiting to see a client.

This technique is best used when sitting comfortably, uncrossing your arms and legs and closing your eyes. Now think of something you want to improve – a skill, a technique or a facet about your personality. For example, let's imagine you want to improve your self-confidence. So decide – do you want to improve it in a way you've never experienced before or do you want to go back to a time when you were much more confident than you are currently? This will become relevant as you will see in a moment. Now with your eyes shut, imagine walking down a corridor with a lift ahead of you.

As you get near the doors of the lift you press the button, the doors open and you step inside. The doors now shut and you notice you are on floor 18. You select B for basement and the lift starts to descend – quite slowly at first. As the lift continues to move, you notice that your arms, legs, neck, shoulders and head are getting heavier yet more relaxed. It's a very pleasant feeling indeed. As this is taking place, the lift continues to descend from floor to floor until eventually you get to the basement. At this point the doors open and you walk out of the lift to see a clock ahead of you. You now have the choice of going to the left of the clock or the right. Going to the left would mean you want to connect with a level of self-confidence you've had before. Going to the right indicates a new level of self-confidence you've never experienced before. This left and right direction is linked with the brain – your left brain is about memory amongst other things, and your right brain is about creativity. Most people will probably choose to go to the right of the clock in order to experience or create something fresh, new and of a higher order.

The clock is relevant as it measures how long you will engage in the process that follows. Notice the time on the clock is your favourite time of day. Okay, so let's imagine you go to the right of the clock into something connected with the most amazing levels of self-confidence. For example, you see yourself mixing with high net worth individuals, highly successful business owners and proprietors and prospects with whom you would love to work. And yet here, with your supreme self-confidence, people are attracted to you as an individual and want to do business with you. You now engage all your senses – you see what's happening, you hear positive things, you engage with the feelings inside you that inspire and motivate you in this situation, and then keep running the scenario through your mind for between two and three minutes.

At the end of this time period, you walk back past the clock and notice an hour has gone by. The significance of the passing hour is that the more you seem to be doing the technique, the more your brain will actually believe that an hour has gone by and therefore is more likely to give you the sense of value as if you had done that technique for a whole hour.

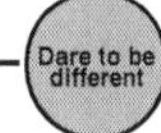

You then walk back towards the lift doors, step inside the lift, and the doors close. You press floor 18 and the lift starts to ascend. As it ascends, your body, in a state of relaxation, starts to 'come to' again. Your head, neck and shoulders, and arms and legs relax. As you count up from basement to 18, you are more aware of your surroundings and feel entirely refreshed from the whole experience. Eventually, at floor 18 you slowly open your eyes.

This technique may take a little getting used to and equally you may not wish do this technique every single day. If you are going to go for this – the most powerful of all MindChangers, then you should use it at least three times a week.

The Train

The Train MindChanger is another non-material technique. This is best used for things you want to change about yourself. Maybe you are less than punctual, are not strong enough in business, or perhaps you are very disorganised. Whatever it is, see yourself (with the traits you want to get rid of) standing on a station platform. However, the image you are seeing of yourself is that of your imaginary twin. You are actually in a train carriage at the platform and you are about to wave your twin brother or sister goodbye. As the train starts to slowly move out of the station, notice how pleased you are leaving behind the person with the trait or traits you really want to change. As the train continues to move at speed, the image of your twin gets smaller and smaller, and as this happens, you notice how pleased you are in waving them goodbye.

This non-material tool is a lot easier to use than the Lift and I strongly recommend that you use either the Lift and/or the Train as one of your MindChanger selection.

Fast Forward

This technique is a lot of fun. The idea is that you select someone to talk to and have a discussion as if it's a year, eighteen months or two years into the future. Obviously, with this in mind you will be discussing things in the past tense – things that have already happened. This makes for a fascinating and often very exciting conversation, even though it does feel strange and uncomfortable to start with. The more you do this technique, the more you'll find that you are positively changing the beliefs you have about your future and you are aligning those beliefs with the real possibility of the results happening for real. You can do this technique on the telephone, by e-mail or face to face. It doesn't have to be for very long on each occasion and you can even do this whilst driving a car completely on your own! By the way, these days if you appear to be talking to yourself whilst driving a car, everyone will assume you are on a hands-free telephone kit – so don't worry. The main thing is to do the technique and start resetting your beliefs.

The Image Diary

The Image Diary is one of my favourites as I'm quite a visual person. Get yourself a quality scrap book and start to paste in pictures of things that you want, either material or non-material. Once you've got a few pages put together, review them by looking at the picture and putting yourself and/or people that are important to you in the picture. You may like to hear your favourite music through headphones at the same time. As with all MindChangers, you can enhance the experience by using as many of your senses as possible.

Avoid cutting pictures from magazines with lots of writing. The pictures should be a picture only without any words attached. Add to your image diary whenever you can and remove pictures once that objective has been achieved.

Flip Cards

Finally, I'd like to conclude with probably the most popular MindChanger of all – the flip cards. Buy yourself some index cards and then write statements of material and non-material origin on the cards, limiting yourself to one goal or objective per card. As always write them up in the past tense and make these statements as interesting and exciting as possible. You should have between twenty and thirty of these cards. If you can't think of that many separate things, then you can have several cards on the same subject to make up the numbers. It's important to have at least twenty, otherwise it's a

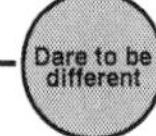

bit like going to the gym and doing two press-ups because that's all you can think of doing. Equally, these are your mental press-ups and you need at least twenty to build your mental strength. Once you have your cards written up, read them once a day and ensure your eyes travel over all the words. Never read a card that's not important to you as all of these cards should be things you want to happen with passion and conviction.

I cannot emphasise how important MindChangers have been to me over the years and I can cite many many stories of how these simple yet powerful psychological tools have made a massive impact on the success of the world's top performers. By using these techniques, you have nothing to lose and and just about everything to gain.

Timings and locations

There is no ideal time to use these techniques because each person will be different. I quite like starting and finishing each day with at least one MindChanger.

You can also do them as often as you choose. However, as a 'rule of thumb', practice at least two techniques once a day. Many of them can be done just about anywhere though given the need to close your eyes for The Lift, I strongly advise against driving at the same time!

The biggest challenge you will face is complacency, particularly after some initial success. You are delighted with early results, and therefore promptly stop doing them! Huge mistake … keep on keeping on using them every day.

You should also vary their use. With the cards, shuffle them so you avoid reading the cards in the same sequence each time. You may like to vary The Lift and The Train, doing one the first day and the other the day after that and so on. Never keep images in your Image Diary if they fail to inspire you – remove them for something else and alter the Walking MindChanger phrase if you are getting bored with it.

You may also like to consider setting up a 'MindChanger Buddy' – someone else who is going to start this process with you. You can support each other and indeed check up on each other once a week.

I've heard the most astounding excuses over the years from people with whom I have shared MindChangers. People would say they could not find the right cards to write their statements on, or they wanted to wait until after their dog had its puppies or their mother-in-law had visited them – or whatever! Get over your self-sabotage by realising what you have to lose and what you have to gain by making this really work.

So, over to you once more. Name your two to three techniques, prepare them if need be, then start … today! It will be one of the best decisions you've ever made. Go for it!

End-of-chapter classic quotes

'You can determine what your future income will be and accomplish it.'

'You have unlimited opportunities for advancement along paths of your own choosing.'

'Habits die hard! What you are or what you do is as the result of habit. You have created what you are today. If you are to change what you become you must form new habits. Either you will form new habits beginning today or your life will continue as in the past.'

'Be understood. Education is only half the battle. Trying to impress upon people how smart you are won't make you successful. Transferring knowledge into concepts that can be easily understood is the key.'

'Network. Create networks and centres of influence. Soon you will develop a reputation for being the expert in a particular field.'

ACTION STEPS

1. Re-read this chapter and commit to at least:

    - 20 mindchanger flipcards
    - trying the walking mindchanger
    - buying some coloured dots and placing them where they are prominent in your home or office
    - using the lift daily for a week
    - finding someone to role play fast-forward
    - starting – and regularly reviewing – your own image diary
    - looking for a mindchanger buddy.

9

The Power of Communicating

It probably stands to reason that if you are a good communicator in business, you are likely to attain the success you desire more quickly. Yet many financial advisers appear to give little thought to the whole art of good communication.

My experience as a public speaker tells me that there are some words and phrases which appear the same, and have a completely different effect on an audience.

There is a list of the top 12 most persuasive words?

- ✓ YOU
- ✓ MONEY
- ✓ SAVE
- ✓ NEW
- ✓ RESULTS
- ✓ EASY
- ✓ HEALTH
- ✓ SAFETY
- ✓ LOVE
- ✓ DISCOVERY
- ✓ PROVEN
- ✓ GUARANTEE

Did You also know that there are words which mean 'A' in theory, but actually mean 'Z' in practice? Allow me to explain.

In the UK, you often see the police notice 'Don't drink and drive'. What's extraordinary about this is that it's actually encouraging

motorists to drink! You see, the mind cannot process a negative as a visual thought. So when you're told don't do something, you still see the thing you're not supposed to do.

Don't think of a blue swan.

So what popped into your mind just now? A blue swan, right? By the way, I use this on e-mails where I want a swift response from someone that I suspect will delay replying. I add a PS to the e-mail saying… 'don't feel you have to reply today'. No prizes for guessing what invariably happens!

Okay, back to the power of words. There are some basic rules you may like to consider when writing to prospects and clients. Indeed, this is useful to introducers, professionals – in fact anyone you wish to influence with integrity.

The 7 Golden Writing Rules

- ✓ Plan what you want to write before you write it.
- ✓ Keep paragraphs short.
- ✓ Write in a conversational manner.
- ✓ Ensure you have a title that grabs attention.
- ✓ There must be a beginning, middle and end.
- ✓ Choose to use a simple word rather than a complex one.
- ✓ Remove the clutter in your words.

These rules will serve you well if you stick by them. You can plan what you want to say using a sheet of paper and a pen – and layout all your thoughts, especially using a mind map if at all possible.

Mindmaps® are the invention of Tony Buzan – investigate this great little technique on the Internet or buy one of his many books on the subject. I can confirm that they will make planning and note taking infinitely more successful.

Some paragraphs can be extremely short!

And that's a good thing if you particularly want to draw attention to the important point you are making. Long paragraphs confuse and bore people which, dare I say, is common in the legal profession.

I often smile at what people are saying in their letters – things they would never say in real life. For example *'Dear Mr Daniels, I enclose the aforementioned documents for your personal perusal'*. Shall I translate? How about:

'Good morning, Mr Daniels (use a first name if possible). Here's the information you wanted to look at...'

The same goes for leaflets, brochures and anything else that goes from your business in words.

Headers and titles are also worth mentioning. Do you remember the movie, *'The Shawshank Redemption'*? If you haven't seen it, I highly recommend it. However did you know it nearly 'bombed' at the box office?

The reason was the title. No one knew what it meant, so wouldn't risk buying a ticket. It was only when the word spread from those who did venture to see it that the movie survived, to become one of the most popular movies of all time.

The next time you send an e-mail or write a letter, especially to a client, ensure you have a title or headline that grabs the attention. It may make the difference between the recipient actually reading your communication or not.

Now, let's look at the process of sending out information to get new business.

Using approach letters

Sometimes it might be preferable to send out an approach letter prior to making an approach phone call. Let's start by considering the shape of the communication itself.

As the two examples show, there's an intrinsic difference in the structure.

The first one consists of two unwieldy paragraphs that look quite a tedious read. In the second, the text is broken up with a couple of one liners … making it far more visually appealing.

To begin the communication, I would always recommend starting with 'Hello' rather than the more formal 'Dear', simply because it's how you'd talk to someone in real life – and it's different. It's amazing how many people do not *dare to be different*, but prefer to stick with accepted traditions and norms. Starting a letter with 'Dear …' comes from Elizabethan times when it was how people spoke to each other in real life.

The best advice for effective written communication is: **make it compelling**. Anything less than compelling is probably a waste of your time and money, and you'd be better off with a phone call.

The NLP factor

The 'science' of NLP (Neuro-Linguistic Programming) was formulated by Dr Richard Bandler and John Grinder in the 1970s. Over the decades, it has become a huge subject, now taught in just

about every country of the world.

I was introduced to NLP a number of years ago and have used it successfully ever since. This is especially the case in situations where I'm trying to build rapport with a new client or professional introducer.

NLP is based on a number of concepts with a fundamental appreciation that we all depend on our five senses, and tend to lean towards one in particular when communicating.

Many people react positively to a visual image or picture. These are the 'visuals' amongst us. The 'auditories' react to the spoken word or sounds or music, and the 'kinaesthetics' are the emotionally-driven where the stimulus is a feeling like a gut reaction.

To use this aspect of NLP effectively, we must first know with which stimulus our prospective 'communicatee' will best align.

It's actually quite easy to find this out. Simply ask a question which the other person will need to think about. Ask, for example, who their teacher was at the first school they attended – and then watch their eyes.

If they are a 'visual', they will tend to look up or appear to be searching for a picture by staring at something. For these people, who will tend to buy a product on its appearance or visual appeal, try using pictures, illustrations or diagrams when you are making a point. In terms of conversation, the visual will use phrases such as, 'I see what you mean', or 'Let's look at it this way' – visual concepts.

Individuals who are 'auditory' will almost certainly look sideways (as if to their ears) so this type of individual will probably most enjoy conversations and the spoken word. They will buy a car, not so much because of its looks or performance, but because of the quality of the CD more like! Or because they were captivated by the dulcet tones of the salesperson and what he or she spoke about. In conversation, they will use phrases such as 'I hear what you are saying', or 'That sounds awful', – hearing concepts.

Kinaesthetics will look down and to their right or straight into your eyes when they think about an answer. How they feel about things will dominate their attention in this process. These people would buy the car for its comfort or the sense of feeling great when sat behind

the wheel. They will say things like, 'It doesn't feel right to me', or 'Let's touch on that again' – feeling concepts.

The way to use this knowledge is to make sure you use seeing, hearing and feeling words in your presentations. This guarantees interest from the person you are communicating with, and is particularly important in group presentations.

Essentially, people communicate best with people who are like them, and when you match people by the words you use or the style in which you communicate, you have the best chance to create high rapport and solidify a relationship/mutual understanding.

Body Language is another subject often associated with communication, and I do advise caution. There are no real hard or fast rules about what body movements or positions may or may not mean, despite the textbooks that state otherwise. Think about it. Have you ever been very interested in talking to someone with their arms folded? It happens a lot, and yet may simply mean the person talking to you is more comfortable like that.

Of course, it may also indicate being defensive or shutting themselves off from you. However, there are two overriding factors;

1 what the person is saying at the time, or what their behaviour in general indicates
2 whether the body movement happened as a result of something you said.

These two factors, when combined with body language concepts, work much better, so I tend to look for any body movement after I say something important. You don't really need to be a body language expert to work out what the 'movement-reaction' meant.

Lies and more lies

Finally in this section, let me tell you how you may be able to tell if someone is not being entirely truthful.

In NLP terms, when someone is asked a question, and they look up or sideways to their right (to your left as you look at them), they are creating an answer because they're accessing the right side of the

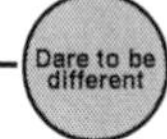

brain – their creative side. This may indicate that they are inventing an answer, whereas if they looked to their left (your right), they are drawing the answer from memory (and thus will probably be speaking the truth). Be careful though – some very honest people like to create the best possible answer and therefore are not necessarily lying.

It is said that people pushing their fingers into their collar or fiddling with clothing may be a sign of not being entirely honest in what they are saying. Watch for the signs, but do not be too literal or invariable in your interpretations.

Rudimentary rapport

To summarise, good communication is about rapport. The basics of rapport can be listed as:

- ☑ Smile!
- ☑ Make eye contact without staring.
- ☑ Remember that people prefer a visual, auditory or kinaesthetic style.
- ☑ Match people's voices in terms of tone, volume and speed without obviously copying them.
- ☑ Refrain from folding your arms or legs when meeting someone for the first time.

It's also good to be mannerly. My experience of cultures with incredibly good manners points to the Far East. It's in this part of the world where I have been most impressed by people's courtesy and good manners. Such behaviour cannot but help create rapport, and so it should be in all we do in life and business. It is something which can be implemented without cost and without delay – but the benefits will be immediate.

End-of-chapter classic quotes

'Work smarter. If you make a sale, don't take time off to celebrate. Instead, look at it as motivation to sell more whilst you are on a roll. Make appointments when your mood is positive. The more people you see the better. Which is better, a hundred percent of twenty deals or twenty percent of a hundred deals.'

'There's always an Apocalypse Du Jour.'

'Whoever said it's not whether you win or lost that counts; probably lost!'

'Life involves constant change – you must change and grow daily, weekly, yearly. If you refuse to grow, you will die. If not physically then emotionally.'

'Winning isn't everything – but wanting to win is.'

'You must recognise your obligations to yourself, to your family, your customer, your company and, most of all, to your prospect.'

'You owe it to your prospect to improve his or her life or business if your product or service can provide the means. You also owe it to yourself, for the sake of your own self image.'

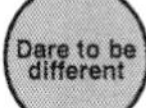

ACTION STEPS

1. **Using this business analysis chart, award a score for each of the business disciplines (adjust these to suit yourself). Commit to doing this analysis every three months – this will help you to focus on the progress you are making. If you are doing well, award yourself.**

   Note – any score that falls into the dark band needs to be addressed immediately; the middle band indicates an acceptable level of performance; and the light band indicates peak performance.

Discipline	Score									
	1	2	3	4	5	6	7	8	9	10
Confidence										
Personal ambition										
Adapting to change										
Persistence										
Taking action										
Order and organisation										
Communication with others										
Personal appearance										
Plans and planning										
Time management										
Daily activity awareness										
Focus										
Dealing with problems										
Happiness and personal contentment										
Physical condition/achievement										
Sales										

10

Creating Business Clarity

Consider if you will the benefits to your business if you could create clarity in all you say, do and strive for. There is so much to say around the idea of sheer simplicity, so I for one am a real advocate of the 'less is more' principle.

In the financial services profession in particular, there seems to be a fixation with increasing turnover, and that the only consistent measure of success is the top line. Why? May I suggest that what we business owners should be concentrating on is margin or baseline profit. After all, that is what any successful business is measured by and it is this aspect that really counts in creating an 'Exit Strategy' or the sale of the business.

Until you have a model in place that clearly and simply allows you to make a profit each month, every month, you don't have a business, you have a liability.

Of course, people can go overboard with this. Those individuals who look to play the 'cut costs at all costs' game, succumb to that dreadful business complaint called customer dispersal. In other words, cutting costs must impact on the quality of your offering to the customer, who in turn looks to other suppliers who offer more to them.

If your customer or client proposition is likely to suffer by cutting costs, you may as well cut your losses now and get a job, because you certainly miss one of the core fundamentals in setting up and running a successful business.

A case in point is my local Indian takeaway.

After previously getting the dishes served up in quality plastic

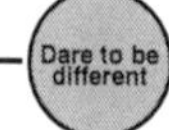

containers marked up with neatly printed labels and free accompaniments, they had clearly gone on a cost-cutting exercise. Suddenly, to my dismay, they were using cardboard containers where some of the food seeped out, the labels were replaced with an illegible written message on each item and there were no more 'freebies'.

Though the food was the same, I have to say I no longer felt a loyalty to this business as I felt cheated – given the prices had not reduced – and eventually I was tempted to go elsewhere. When I found a competitor's packaging and general image more customer-focused, I ended up moving my business – and I am know I was not the only one to do this, as the business later failed. So all the cost-cutting to boost profits worked against the business big time!

It's astonishing to meet so many people who continue to struggle with a business they're not really in control of.

The formula for success here is surely all about a healthy balance between expenditure and turnover that creates a profit that's worth all the hard work and effort.

I remember getting a call from a new prospect who lived one hundred and fifteen miles away. This lady had been recommended by an existing client, and I was of course delighted to get the enquiry. However, it soon became evident that in doing the work she was requesting, I would make a very small amount. When I worked out my hourly rate, travel expenses and what I could alternatively spend the six hours and thirty five minutes on, I soon realised this had to be done another way.

So, I contacted a competitor! And by asking him to do the business locally and split the commission with me, my few moments on the telephone with my prospect netted me £48. I also got to keep the client long term, and she even called my office to thank me for the prompt service and assistance. Some months later she offered me some more work which was profitable enough for me to handle the matter personally.

The problem is we don't tend to concentrate on our strengths because, even though we clearly need to at times, it seems difficult to delegate.

Less is more, and business clarity is about doing the right things in

the most effective way at the right time.

If we analysed the way we conducted our business in detail, we would probably find dozens and dozens of tasks that demand our time but very few that have a positive commercial impact.

So the question is … do you want to *survive* or *thrive*?

Attempting to be all things to all people never works. There is of course nothing wrong with offering a comprehensive service but it is important to know (a) what we can deliver effectively and profitably, and (b) those things which need delegating or outsourcing.

Creating a client offering

An important step towards business clarity is knowing what you do for your clients. In other words, what is your 'client offering'.

Remember the last time you were asked by someone what you did for a living? What did you say? Like me, if you've ever found yourself in the challenging position of not wanting to say *'I'm a life insurance salesperson'*, but couldn't think of an alternative, consider the following…

Imagine, for the moment, you are in an elevator that stopped at each of three floors, before you get out at the fourth. The first floor sees the owner of a small business get into the elevator. *'What do you do for a living?'* he asks. *'I help business owners protect their assets from creditors and I show them how to increase, protect and preserve their wealth,'* you reply.

At the next floor a lady who is obviously approaching retirement, but also appears to be a person of some financial means, steps into the elevator. *'What do you do for a living?'* she asks. *'I'm a Wealth Preservation specialist. I specialise in tax mitigation and estate planning so that individuals can get the best for themselves and for their intended beneficiaries.'*

At the third floor a lady of about 35 steps into the elevator with you. *'What do you do for a living?'* she asks. *'I help my clients, most of whom have children, to reduce or eliminate their debts, plan for future events such as school fees or other future goals and I start to help them design a wealth creation strategy for the future.'*

For a variety of reasons, we can sometimes feel uncomfortable

referring to ourselves by a particular title, maybe because we don't wish to be labelled.

In the example above we have been asked the same question three times but on each occasion have given different answers. The truth of the matter is that we are specialists in all these areas but we need to position ourselves by responding not just to a clearly identified requirement, but also talking a language to which another person will most easily relate.

For example, it is no good talking about life insurance to a retired person unless it's to deal with estate taxes, any more than we would talk about wealth management to someone who clearly struggles to survive financially.

We all fear rejection which is why, when confronted with a question like 'What do you do for a living?', we would probably rather say nothing than come out with an inappropriate answer. So think about communicating in a way that is far more likely to create a positive response while still giving a clarity to your customer?

From a 'less is more' perspective, always have a clear, concise and simple fallback position. So with business owners I tend to favour 'business growth specialist' and with a high net worth individual I prefer 'wealth creation planner'. It's not really difficult, as long as you give it some thought.

Another area in which we tend to have challenges is calling on people we know.

In the early days, despite what my manager told me, I was always trying to avoid calling my friends and family because I didn't know how they would react to an approach to do business although I was never able to explain why I had such a fear of contacting those closest to me. However, it then dawned on me that anyone who became a client or was prepared to endorse the services I provided to others was in fact a very valuable business asset!

The Client Ladder

Several years ago, I was speaking to my accountant – a tax adviser with whom I had worked for many years. Such was the level of his expertise, he received not just a number of introductions from me but would also generate a large percentage of his new clients from advertising and client referrals. Despite the pressures of an ever-increasing workload, he was doing well.

Over a period of time, the quality of service he was providing started to diminish. He was spending more and more time with clients who were clearly not profitable for his business. In turn, he was neglecting his very wealthy clients who ran their own successful businesses. By now he was starting to recognise the problems and so called me in one morning for a coffee. He wanted to know how he might continue to build his 'top line' whilst eliminating the expense of dealing with fairly non-profitable clients.

My answer to him was simple. I told him to double his fees.

His response, not untypical of most people who cannot see that 'less is more', was, *'But I would lose half my clients!'*

Think about this response. Double his fees and lose half his clients. Where's the problem?

I told him that when I was a manager of a large life assurance company, every day I would come across associates hoarding hundreds of client files because they somehow felt reassured that by having a large number of clients they could ensure success.

Forgive me for pointing out the obvious, but our clients will not take the trouble to contact us unless we fulfil the first promise we ever make… to create a long-term relationship built on professional trust.

I would argue that we cannot possibly regard clients as potential sources of new business when it has been a number of years since we saw them last. These people are not prospects, they are suspects and if they have no loyalty towards us, they will turn out to be a business liability, rather than a strategic asset.

It is not about numbers, it is about quality.

Fifty clients who perfectly fit the type of profile of the individual we want to build a relationship with is infinitely better than a list of one thousand names and addresses. Yet one of the most repeatedly asked questions in our profession is 'How do I obtain more clients?' How about changing your mindset and think about:

'How do I obtain more quality clients?'

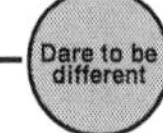

Building a great business is about targeting those people who can really add value to what we already have in place, which is why the 'Top Twenty Clients' idea really works so well.

Identifying your **'Top Twenty Clients'** (although this number can be higher if you wish) achieves two things.

1. You will end up building an even better relationship with these people to the point where you can speak with them more openly and honestly.
2. Less is more. It's easier to do business with these clients and so much easier to get personal introductions from them – who, by the way, are likely to be of similar high quality.

As we know, the less time we spend looking for new clients, the more time we can dedicate to providing a superb level of service all round.

Once you have your Top Twenty off to a fine art, you might then like to create a *Client Ladder*.

This simply involves creating parameters within your business such as the number of clients you will have at any one time. More clarity and simplicity!

Now the goal is to find new clients who are good enough to sit within the boundaries you have set.

For example, let's say we decide to work with a maximum of 100 clients rather than twenty, and a personal introduction is made by one of them.

If the recommended individual doesn't offer you the same business opportunity as an existing 'Top 100' client, then you would simply not be able to take them on. Instead, you might pass them to another adviser for a split of the commission or fee.

Conversely, if a new prospective client is introduced and it is someone with whom we wish to build a business relationship, then we have to delegate the client at the very bottom of the ladder to another colleague – maybe a junior adviser or paraplanner.

There will be the occasions when you also decide to 'sack' a client because he or she no longer requires a service or has not contacted you for a number of years.

You will also find more people aspiring to become one of your 'Top 100' clients, simply because of the exclusivity of what they see as a 'club'. If clients appreciate the quality and caring service being provided, they will constantly ask what they need to do to remain a client.

So let's consider for a moment, what your new ideal 'less is more' business might look like.

First, you might wish to insist that all clients have a minimum income of $75,000 per annum (£50,000) or they have a net wealth of at least $1 million (£600,000). Taking this approach means more interest in your practice, not less. They are also clearer about your client proposition and have something to boast about in front of their friends … which in turn gets the message out about your specialist and quality business.

Once it has been decided whether or not you really want this person in your Top 100, I would suggest you need to look at the following.

The primary consideration must be to help clients see very clearly, where they are now, especially in financial terms, before you look at where they want to be at some future date. Now you can start to construct a plan in order to bridge the identified gap.

Whether or not a fee is charged for the first meeting can be discussed at this stage, but I feel it is appropriate to deal comprehensively with the difference between fee-based and commission-based advice up front. Personally, I believe that charging fees will play a large part in the future of financial services. If you are not charging any, I urge you to look at this as soon as possible.

At the end of the meeting – and if the prospective client seems likely to be suitable for your Top 100 – then the appropriate agreements can be signed and the next meeting set.

Building a successful business practice is about achieving strategic business goals, not just about trying hard.

Providing a comprehensive and quality service will generate fantastic results. Communicating your message, clearly and often, will help you acquire many new client opportunities and people will certainly want to become your client if they know what you do in the simplest of terms.

Are you clear about your success?

Let's imagine you are one of thirty associates in your company and your goal is to be number one. As there can only be one top adviser, does this mean that everyone who does not make it to the pinnacle is a failure?

Of course not.

Success is not a comparison of one person to another, success is a comparison of an individual's achievements compared with his or her own potential.

An individual does not have the right to judge another based on their definition of success and in the same way we don't have the right to judge others.

However, there's a major factor that separates successful people from the rest: *they do many of the things they don't really like doing, but do them anyway, in order to get the things they want.*

People who fail still want these same things but won't do the things necessary to get them. They are motivated by comfort zones.

Ask yourself how many things you are willing to go without in your life assuming you knew that, by doing so, you could not fail?

Most people hate being a 'front seater' in life as it's far more comfortable sitting at the back, out of the spotlight, risk-free.

Success then is clear. It's about the progressive and ultimate realisation of a worthwhile predetermined goal or set of goals.

I have a note written at the front of my diary that summarises this concept. It says:

I'll never fail unless I stop taking the next step.

Success is a personal thing. It means different things to different people. Yet clarity and success itself can only emerge from knowing what's important to you. To achieve your own level of success, you

must first recognise that you are an individual and as such, different from every other person. Your wants are different, your needs are different, your problems are different and your destiny is different.

Therefore, your goals must be different too! We must stop looking back and instead take responsibility for where we are and where we want to go in our lives starting from today.

I once read an article that was based on a study of millionaires. The study sought to determine commonalities between these ultra-successful individuals. Some of the characteristics identified are:

- ✓ the ability to cut through to the core of the problem and take charge of a situation quickly.
- ✓ the habit of positive actions consistently
- ✓ effective working rather than hard working
- ✓ enthusiasm at all times
- ✓ a definite and vivid set of persistently visualised goals
- ✓ physically fit
- ✓ giving more than they take
- ✓ learning from adversity
- ✓ strong commitment to their objectives
- ✓ willing to take risks when necessary
- ✓ confident in themselves.

As you know by now, we all have these attributes. The trouble is, we don't fully believe it. That's why MindChangers can make such a radical difference to you.

More than any other previous chapter, I strongly advise you to take the Action Steps that follow. Where some of the post chapter Action Steps may appear optional, *these are compulsory* – if you are serious about your ultimate success. So take a look at them, and please – do it now!

End-of-chapter classic quotes

'Commitment in every activity, especially professional selling, is one of the most important ingredients necessary if you are to succeed and be content in your success. We live by choice, not by chance.'

'Attitude is a choice, the most important one you will ever make.'

'Habits are the key to all success.'

'Kind words cost little, but accomplish much.'

'Real motivation comes from within.'

'Goals are dreams with deadlines.'

'No-one else can raise your self-esteem.'

'No-one was ever heard to say on the death bed, "I wish I had spent more time at the office!"'

'If we listen to them when they are five, six or seven years old, they may listen to us when they are fifteen, sixteen or seventeen.'

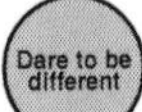

ACTION STEPS

1. Decide how many clients you can realistically manage personally. Create a business ladder and decide upon the parameters of that ladder.

2. Write to, or call, all your 'ladder' clients in order to explain what you want from them and what you will provide, in terms of service, in return.

3. Clear all the names and tasks from your diary or work sheet that have been there for more than three months. Names in the diary for more than three months are no longer prospects, but suspects.

4. Make a list of all the things you know you can delegate to someone else – and do it now.

5. Try to cut down your working day by one hour initially and then, eventually, take one day off every week. You'll still find time to get everything done.

6. In less than 25 words, what is your major purpose in life?

7. Evaluate, again, your strengths and weaknesses and commit to improving at least one area over the next 30 days.

8. Consider ways you can add in greater value to your business proposition – and implement the plan now.

11

The Seven Deadly Sins

Having looked at a number of key strategies and ideas to help in the development of a successful business practice, let's look, for a moment at the things we should definitely be trying to avoid if we are to reach those goals.

First Deadly Sin: No order or organisation

I have often heard the phrase 'tidy life, tidy mind' and I am sure it's true. Sometimes people love disorder mainly because they can then hide in it and look very busy! An untidy desk, cluttered diary, dishevelled appearance or disregard for the importance of punctuality betrays the individual who's not in control of his or her business, mind or life.

Most of us hate paperwork but we have to embrace the administrative process and adopt high standards as a route to an achievable sustainable goal. And if we're the entrepreneurial type of person who has no time to be orderly and organised we have to invest in a good quality personal assistant who can achieve these critical standards on our behalf.

I remember visiting a PR business some years ago at a trade show. I was impressed by their stand and brand image. Picking up their details I found myself driving past their office one day, so I thought I'd drop by unannounced. Was I in for a shock!

Their reception looked like it had been attacked by a plague of boxes. Okay, they were boxes of leaflets for some campaign they appeared to be running, but it felt unprofessional and disorganised. They showed me into this very run-down waiting room, which needed redecorating and the benefit of a carpet cleaner. The manager who came out to greet me had an open shirt and could have done with a shave. His eyes looked bloodshot and his breath smelled of what was obviously the previous night's takeaway..

My time there was brief and I could not get out fast enough… and needless to say I haven't been back, despite their calls to my secretary. Whatever your business – and it's astonishing they were in PR and marketing – order and organisation is crucial.

A few simple tips would be:

- ☑ Work from a clear desk. Keep your desk space tidy at the end of the day and reasonable during the day – especially if you have visitors.
- ☑ Work from a tidy and organised office with a good standard of decor.
- ☑ Systemise everything you can. Leave nothing to chance in building your business.
- ☑ Ensure information is properly stored, indexed and accessible
- ☑ Less paper is better than more paper.
- ☑ Remove any clutter. If in doubt, throw it out.

Second Deadly Sin: No Masterplan

Ask yourself whether your business runs you or whether you run it? Do you know when you are going to exit the business – maybe through retirement or trade sale. Or do you just run ever faster each day to keep up with the changing demands of your profession?

I strongly urge you plan an escape route – even if you decide to stay on and never use it. It also goes without saying that a business without a robust strategy is like a rowing boat without oars.

Creating a Masterplan sounds the most obvious idea in the world but you would be surprised how many financial advisers think of themselves in a job rather than in a business of their own. Even if you are part of a major company, you are still running a business within a business and indeed this type of thinking is key if you are to be successful in your endeavours.

So how do you create a Masterplan? A Masterplan has the following elements:

- a **Vision** – what the 'end game' looks like
- a **Mission** – what needs to be done in order to attain the vision
- a **Strategy** – a day-to-day plan underpinned by a tactical road map that will achieve the Vision and Mission.

There are other questions you need to answer.

? What do you want to achieve?
? What does it look like?
? When do you want it by?
? Why is it so important?
? How will you know you've got there?
? How are you going to start?
? How will you ensure you get to the desired outcome?
? Who will help you or be involved?
? What if there are barriers to your success?
? Do you have alternative plans if need be?

When I first considered my own Masterplan I was not, at that point, convinced of its value. I can only emphasise that not only does it work, but my original plan has been rewritten many times over with the Masterplan continuing to be the 'spine' or basis for the success I have generated by its consistent implementation.

Third Deadly Sin: No hotel days

If you are serious about implementing either the ideas in this book or your own ideas, then you need time for reflection and to plan your ultimate success. I strongly advise you to allocate some time each month, at least to start with, for a *hotel day*. This is such a simple yet very powerful idea that really does make an impact.

Find a location such as a quality hotel, a health club – or even an art gallery – where you can lose yourself for half a day (or all day), then have a brainstorm session with… yourself!

I know when I first did this myself I thought it would only last about half an hour, after which I would get bored. In fact, the opposite was true.

There are some simple rules:

- ✓ Leave your mobile in the car.
- ✓ Tell no one where you are going, though you could leave an emergency number with your PA perhaps or someone trustworthy who will only call you if there is a crisis of such devastating consequences that it cannot wait until later.
- ✓ Only bring documents that are relevant to the brainstorm and planning session.
- ✓ Bring plenty of paper – large sheets are best – and coloured pens.
- ✓ Be 'up to speed' on mindmapping techniques, as developed by Tony Buzan.

I actually found that once you get into this high-level planning session, your mind opens to some of the most amazing thoughts and ideas. I can confirm that I attribute much of my recent success to working 'on' my business rather than working 'in' it like the majority of people do. This is definitely an 'on' technique.

Fourth Deadly Sin: No primary purpose

Every successful individual in the world will tell you that knowing your primary purpose is one of the key ingredients to a totally satisfactory form of success.

You might wonder why this is listed fourth, not first. If it is put first, some people take forever to get their success map going because they want to deliberate for far too long on this one. And I admit it can be tough to work out the answer to:

What is my Primary Purpose in life?

For those of you who are familiar with the successful British entrepreneur, Richard Branson, you might wonder if what drives him

is simple business goals around his successful airline for example, or is it more associated with his hot air ballooning or creating a space trip in the next decade?

What is for certain, is that without a successful business, he would not have the resources for the more unusual pursuits that spur him on.

So what's yours?

If you find that you can answer this – then you are very fortunate. The majority of humans have no idea, and many have not even considered the question. If you can get to the answer, the benefit is immense. It motivates and aligns you in almost every conceivable way.

I suggest you never tell lots of people what your aim is. It's personal, and not for general consumption. What I can say about my own however is that everything I now do revolves around speaking, writing, running my financial services business and spending time pursuing my personal family goals, in a way which inspires and motivates.

As a final note on Primary Purpose, I suggest you ensure that you can convey what you ultimately want in a short sentence. Any primary purpose is straightforward and not complex in its nature. For Ghandi it was perhaps giving India its freedom. For Florence Nightingale it was taking nursing to new levels and for Muhammad Ali it was becoming the best boxer in the world. Of course your primary purpose need not be so grand, but it needs to be thought about and identified. Knowing creates instant personal power and creates an exciting future.

Fifth Deadly Sin: No balance

Being a slave to your business or your favourite leisure activity is an imbalance that will steal your future plans and never give them back. Though there are examples of individuals being very committed to their work and also getting great results, I can also show you the statistics of broken marriages, estranged children and dare I mention – suicides.

If there is no balance in your life, it can't be that much fun.

Planning the other side of business – your personal and family life – is as important as the plans for the business itself.

I woke up to this fact a long time ago and ensure I still do things like take my children to school despite a busy schedule, have many short but quality breaks, and play golf during the week rather than at weekends.

Currently, I run my business on a three to three and a half days a week basis, and this 'less is more' principle stands me in good stead.

The way to make this work is to start booking things in your diary as a bona fide business meeting, such as for example, taking your children to school, registering for a mid-week golf competition or taking time out to pursue a favourite hobby. After all, it is working 'on' your life rather than 'in' it. The balance you create in your life will give you a healthier outlook and reduce the stress. And if there's no respite in your daily activities, what is it all about anyway?

Working effectively and playing effectively was one of my early MindChangers, and I'm delighted to say it came to pass sooner than later.

Sixth Deadly Sin: No integrity

This is not just about the way we conduct ourselves as professionals but the way we are with ourselves. How often do we break promises to ourselves, to those we love or to our clients?

I have always seen integrity as black and white without any shades of grey. Unfortunately there are too many people who have other ideas and for them I am sorry. However,as a financial professional, I would say having no integrity is like having no ink in your pen.

So often we make up our own rules around honesty and doing what's right. Take speeding in a car for example. Many would say this doesn't count or that it's okay to exceed the speed limit when you are in a hurry. If you have agreed to obey traffic rules, I would suggest your integrity is compromised if you then choose to interpret the law to suit yourself.

I wish I could say that I did everything exactly right in life – and

my integrity would be in tatters if I did make such a statement! However, I do make a point of ensuring that I do know the difference between doing something with integrity and doing something without. So if I choose to park my car in a location with a restricted parking notice, even for two minutes, and my vehicle is involved in an accident, then I have only myself to blame – I can't transfer the blame to anyone else – as I accepted full responsibility for my actions.

Equally, in business – I always try to put myself in the client's shoes and treat them as I would want to be treated. I have noticed that the more I do this, the more business I get in the form of recommendations and personal introductions. I went a garage some years ago to get a problem on my car fixed. Thinking it was a major repair, I requested the work be done – only to be told that it was in fact very minor and the car would be ready in ten minutes. I was astonished, realising the garage owner could easily have booked my vehicle in for the expensive job and I would have been none the wiser. However, I told this story to many people, most of whom asked me for the garage's contact details. I must have sent that garage thousands of pounds' worth of business over the years.

So what's your integrity like in your business? Remember – you can't have a bit of integrity. Either you have it, or you haven't. It's black and white – there is no grey. The ideal is to keep working on it in order to get it as perfect as possible – it will pay immense dividends many times over.

Seventh Deadly Sin: Not going through the 'Front Door'

The front door in life involves commitment and a determination to meet problems head on. Using the back door is the easy way in because we can often pass through it unnoticed. To truly succeed we sometimes need to understand there is no gain without pain.

Dealing with the problems and issues that everyday life throws at us has never been easy, nor will it get any easier. But as human beings we have an in-built mechanism which is designed to self-preserve.

Think about the stories we have all read in the newspapers about

the mother, 120lb in weight, who single-handedly lifted a motor car to free her trapped child underneath? Consider those that suffer terrible illness or appalling injuries and, immediately and radically, have to adapt to their new circumstances in order to survive. If we did not possess this ability to fight in the face of difficulty, these things would simply not happen.

These stories, or a personal experience like them, put the challenges we all face, every day, into some sort of perspective. Is contacting our Top 20 clients and asking them for help in developing our business contacts so difficult? What stops us making the telephone call that might be the start of a great new relationship with a client? What stops us filling our diary with new meetings with higher net worth prospects and businesses? What prevents us fulfilling our dreams and ambitions?

Whilst I think we all search for more answers to life's questions, one thing is for certain – only we can determine our own future and only we can make a difference to the relatively short time we are here.

**And by the way, if you risk nothing,
you could be risking everything.**

End-of-chapter classic quotes

'How can you expect to fly with the eagles when you are scratching about with the turkeys?'

'It ain't a sin if you crack a few laws now and then, just as long as you don't break any.'

'Doing something almost right is useless – it's doing it exactly right that matters.'

'The easiest way to make money is to stop losing it.'

'Attitude is a choice – the most important one you will ever make.'

'Habits are the key to all success.'

'Goals are just dreams with deadlines.'

'No one else can raise your self-esteem.'

ACTION STEPS

1. Set yourself a goal to make at least ten calls you've been meaning to make for a while. Mark yourself out of ten for each call – 3 for picking up the receiver; 3 for dialling the number; 3 for speaking to the person; and 1 for a 'yes' or 'no'. Reward yourself for a score of 90 or better.

2. Scan review this book and highlight the words, sentences, quotes or activities which you feel will make a difference to your performance. Commit to reviewing these often and become accountable to yourself by telling someone else what you intend to do, now that you have decided your route to outstanding success.

12

When Life Throws Down the Gauntlet

I've always viewed problems as challenges, and yet sometimes people smile at this idea. *'Why don't you be truthful with yourself?'* they say. *'It's a problem you have, and there's no getting away from it.'* And of course that's just their perspective.

Quite simply, I have chosen another view of life. You see, when you call a problem a challenge, your brain goes into a different mode of thinking ... one of solution, not frustration. You've selected the command button to retrieve an answer rather than sit with an issue, pampering it so it doesn't want to go away.

If you are already achieving everything you've set out to achieve with your business and life as a whole, then congratulations. But I rather suspect the reason you've invested in this book is because there are still things that are missing. If that is the case then I have a very poignant question for you.

How long do you want to live like this?

Being able to deal with challenges swiftly and successfully is an important part of running a successful business and life, particularly when, for most of us, our businesses and lives are inextricably linked.

For most of us, the events in New York and Washington on 11th September 2001 and in London on 7th July 2005 will live with us vividly for the rest of our lives. But despite the terrible loss of life and the continuing problems those tragic events still cause, most people always seem to find a way of bouncing back. Human beings are surprisingly resilient, particularly in the face of adversity.

I am sure we can all think of many events throughout the course of history that could have changed our lives or that did, in fact, shape our destiny. When I hear people complaining about the inadequacies of life and all the things that are seemingly working against them, I ask that they put their problems into context.

Those that have achieved any level of success have done so because of a fierce determination to succeed in spite of the occasional difficulty. One of the most uplifting experiences of my life was meeting Mark Peck, a much respected international speaker and trusted financial professional whose parents were told, when he was just three months old, that he was not expected to live long and that for the period of time he did live, he would be a helpless cripple.

Now married and with a family, Mark still remains philosophical about his severe disabilities. He recounted, in a fabulous speech he made at both the Million Dollar Round Table meeting and Life Insurance Association (UK) Convention, that without those experiences he wouldn't be Mark Peck.

I'm sure we all know someone who has suffered through severe ill health, bankruptcy or the death of a loved one, but we really do have an in-built mechanism that helps us cope, adapt and even succeed in spite of those challenges. Sometimes, we just don't realise that we have such strength and resilience.

Being strong and maintaining that strength is tough. Being a good leader, a business owner, a parent or someone who simply remains committed to the achievement of his or her goals is also tough. But no-one said it was easy.

The individual who I can now call my very best client did not ask me to work with him until I had been thrown out of his office for the third time!

I didn't see this as rejection but I did recognise the challenge. I knew there was a business opportunity and good reason he needed to work with me, but I also knew I had to gain his trust and if I was prepared to fight the challenge in order to win the battle, I would eventually achieve this…and I am pleased to say I did. Looking back, no one would have blamed me for walking away. Indeed I can

imagine many people advising me after the second knock back that I had done all I could and it was time to move on.

An important point here is the idea that if something doesn't work, change what you are doing. Some people take this to mean giving up. I've learned that it means tackling the same challenge from a different perspective. Use a different approach, a different route or a different idea – but stick with the same persistence, patience and enthusiasm.

Most times, things don't get handed to us on a plate; we have to put up a fight. As we have already discussed, the challenges in life are just nature's way of testing our level of commitment. But if we think of it as a problem or stumbling block, rather than a stepping stone, we're in trouble from the start with no bridge to circumvent the obstacle.

Funnily enough, children tend not to struggle with the same things adults do. For the reasons outlined earlier, they have not yet formed opinions or reached conclusions about what we perceive to be positive or negative factors – which are largely based on experience. Having spent three years as a manager within a large organisation, I am now firmly of the opinion that challenges are just another 'excuse for failure' hook that many people choose to hang their coat on. Some people focus on problems and complain about them for the simple reason that it's much easier to moan than to eliminate the challenge and move forward. The biggest challenge that most of us face is change.

As human beings, we are driven to seek control over our environment. We like to be able to predict with some certainty what will happen when we take action and therefore be empowered to act.

When we're in control, we feel confident – and confidence is incredibly important. Therefore we are comfortable with all the things we know how to do including, possibly, the ability to make a phone call to a prospect, to open or close a sale, to deal with a difficult client or to persist in the face of rejection and ask for a personal recommendation.

Whatever changes we have to face, there will always be core elements of the new regime or environment we can feel confident in addressing. So, again, focus on the positive elements. In other words, think about what you can achieve and attempt to eliminate – possibly

by delegating the weaknesses. In the same way a skilled mountaineer would not attempt to scale a mountain in one climb but would rather set a strategy to form a base camp and then climb in stages from that point. Identifying what we can deal with in small steps and then taking positive action, step by step, will overcome even the things we previously saw as impossible tasks. *'A journey of a thousand miles starts with a single step'.*

Motivation and persistence are great attributes to have when dealing with change. (I refer you to the use of MindChangers). In the same way that athletes map out their annual calendar, selecting the events they need to enter, then planning and managing their performance and activities according to their goals, so we should be looking to do the same. Good planning establishes very clear goals and enables us to remain focused. This, in turn, maximises our chances of success. It is also worth noting that changes within our own environment can also affect those of either our family or clients. So, if others are used to us working in a certain way, then we need to be especially careful in how we manage change, so that it has minimal impact on those people.

The perceived pain associated with running a business is not necessarily just about managing change. Having to pick up the telephone to make contact with a prospective client whilst knowing there's every likelihood that we may get rejected is an ability that we all naturally possess, it's just that we haven't honed the skill we need to achieve a successful outcome.

Top tips for dealing with challenges

- ✓ Break the challenge down into simple steps.
- ✓ Action the steps in the right sequence.
- ✓ Take action immediately rather than procrastinate (otherwise the challenge grows…)
- ✓ Free your mind by thinking 'vertically' as well as 'horizontally', or by 'thinking outside the box' as they say.
- ✓ Get the information that could offer you more solutions or options.

- ✓ Organise a 'brainshare' session with one or more other people to help you with the challenge. Remember that your challenge will not have the same emotional connection for someone else who invariably can see the solution more clearly than you.
- ✓ Compare! When you compare your challenge with what others are facing around the world – it often puts things into a more manageable perspective.

Diverting future challenges

Many people in selling have challenges with their family life because of the pressure and stress associated with business.

We have a large wall-mounted map of the world – and each time I travel, the children put a coloured pin in the place where I will be working. It's a fun way to connect them to my trip and also to see how many places I have visited. Involving your family in what you do and getting their 'buy-in' is so important. If you fail to communicate with your partner and family and share your challenges, you are often creating yet another challenge. We are all aware of the pain around family challenges so take every opportunity to avoid causing them.

The classic 'Elephant on the Horizon' story is worth mentioning here. If you imagine an elephant on the horizon, it seems so tiny. Yet close up, a few steps away from you, the animal looks enormous.

Now imagine this is a diary.

When you plan well in advance, things are easy to deal with because the task (the elephant) is on the horizon – it's small and easily manageable. So, if you are not constantly managing the situation, the 'elephant' ends up looking at you between the eyes from a couple of yards away, and there's little you can do at the last moment. So, I suggest that planning well in advance is a key factor.

The challenges around travelling

Here are some travel tips to help minimise the stress of business travel on both traveller and family.

- ✓ Carefully analyse the purpose of each trip and say 'no' to unnecessary ones.

- ✓ Draw travel 'boundaries' as a family, deciding how much travel is excessive.
- ✓ Maintain reasonable intervals between trips, if possible.
- ✓ If you are married with a family, travel on weekdays where business trips are concerned – if you are single travel on weekends.
- ✓ Travel on special occasions such as birthdays and anniversaries at your peril!
- ✓ Telephone home each day.
- ✓ Take one hour off to be alone each busy business day when you're on the road, so you may relax, exercise or do something new and different.
- ✓ Schedule weekly relationship time in your diary.
- ✓ Take loved ones on business trips occasionally.
- ✓ When you come home, listen to the family first before you share your own news of your trip.

Children love receiving letters and e-mails. If you have to be away from home, drop them a line. Telling your children that you love them and showing physical affection as often as possible is also a basic human need and moulds, to a considerable extent, the character of your child.

The big question is whether we work long hours irrespective of need. How often do we find ourselves passing up the opportunity to read a story to our children or spend time with other members of our family because we simply thought we had to 'finish a job off?'

Whilst business matters may be a tremendous burden from time to time there is always space in the day or week to develop family traditions, setting aside an evening where the whole family sits around the dinner table. Or a Sunday afternoon stroll? Or a 'picnic' night when the children get to choose what they want to eat?

Rob Parsons, one of the best speakers I have ever heard on the subject of balancing business and family time, has been a tremendous source of inspiration; to the point where I now see the real value in spending as much time as possible with those that are dear to me.

Remember, if your child is ten years old, 3,650 days have already

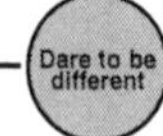

gone – you have only 2,920 left before they leave home. Sobering thought isn't it?

Think of all the urgent calls you have ever received or the tasks you were asked to do – were any of them so urgent they couldn't wait at least five minutes? Avoid saying things things like, *'There will soon be a time when I can slow down'*, or *'I'm working as hard as I am for the kids.'* As Rob Parsons says, *'By trying to give our kids what we didn't have, we forget to give them what we did have.'*

I have experienced a quite an amazing transformation in the behaviour and general relationship I have with my children simply because I tell them things like I believe in them and that I constantly try to catch them doing something right, rather than wrong.

The same is true in business. Colleagues, clients and other business associates will always react far more positively and be more committed to helping us grow and develop if we adopt these same basic principles in the relationship.

Ask yourself what you would want to do differently if you were married to yourself. Perhaps even, what you would do if you knew this was your last day on earth. Many of us will not be fortunate enough to live a long and fulfilling life so why take the chance of not living each day in the best possible way?

If we had a sense of urgency, remained focused and could achieve something approaching a sensible balance in life, how good would we feel?

So I have to ask the question, why isn't this happening already or why can't it happen at this point?

To start with, consider the following 11-point process and if you can't think of any good reasons not to implement and action them today, then please at lest give them a try:

1. **What have I accomplished so far?** Reviewing and acknowledging your past successes are very important to maintain confidence levels and to fuel desire and determination.

2. **What has been my biggest disappointment?** Putting this into perspective, especially with regard to successes achieved, can

often lead to the conclusion that things aren't quite as bad as was first envisaged.

3. **What have I learned?** We all make mistakes and have disappointments but these are all good experiences if the lessons to be learned from them are turned into plans to prevent the same mistake happening again.

4. **How do I limit myself and how can I stop?** As individuals we are the only ones to restrict our success.

5. **What are my personal values?** Most of us feel better if we are doing things we perceive to be good.

6. **What is my role in life?** Failed success can provide the ability to have the things you want but balance is equally important. You cannot put your life 'on hold' whilst you decide.

7. **What will I focus on next?** Knowing that you have the ideas and strategies to always get what you focus on helps build a determined way of generating results.

8. **What are my goals?** There is nothing wrong with setting the highest goals; especially when you can justify it by reaching the target. The main attention of your focus (the goals) may be something quite challenging but break it down into small manageable pieces and start from there.

9. **What are my top seven goals?** Use the 7:4:1 method, described earlier in this book, to help make achievement and results attainable.

10. **How can I achieve those results?** Part of the plan is confidence and this only comes from practice. Keep persevering with all the best ideas you currently have and then add some more (maybe from this book?) in order to achieve a successful outcome. Too

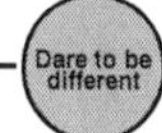

many of us spend all our time focusing on problems when, in fact, we should be spending no more than 10% of our time on the problems and 90% of our time on the solution.

11. And the classic question of all time…**'If I knew I could not fail, what goal would I embark on right now?'**

There is no doubt that creating synergy in life, including work family and health, can have a positive influence on production. When we have balance in our lives, everything we do, we do better. And if we think all of this is impossible, then let's consider, from time to time, going back to basics. Sometimes there is more fulfilment to be had in life by stepping sideways, or even backwards, so long as we subscribe to the theory we should be setting personal goals before business goals. Success is more than making money. Successful people know this because they don't find time, they *make* time. Life is so much simpler when we know what is essential.

The story of the carpenter

Isn't it strange how we seem to set much higher standards for ourselves than for others? At this point, I am reminded of a story about an elderly carpenter, which illustrates this point:

> An elderly carpenter was ready to retire. He told his employer of his plans to leave the house-building business and live a more leisurely life with his wife, enjoying his extended family. He would miss the pay-cheque, but he needed to retire. They could get by.
>
> The contractor was sorry to see his good worker go and asked if he could build one more house as a personal favour. The carpenter said yes, but in time it was easy to see that his heart was not in his work. He allowed his workmanship to become shoddy and he started to use inferior materials. It was an unfortunate way to end a dedicated career.
>
> When the carpenter finished his work, the employer came to inspect the house. He handed the front-door key to the

carpenter and said, *'My gift to you'.* The carpenter was shocked. What a shame! If only he had known he was building his own house, he would have done it all so differently.

So it is with us. We build our lives, a day at a time, often putting less than our best into the building. Then, with a shock, we realise we have to live in the house we have built. If we could do it all over again, we would do it so differently. But we cannot go back.

You are the carpenter. Each day you hammer a nail, place a board or erect a wall. Life is a do-it-yourself project. Your attitudes and the choices you make today builds the house you live in tomorrow. So build wisely!

End-of chapter classic quotes

'Strength is the end point of a mental process, not the starting point of a physical one.'

'Strength is something that comes from the fear of being beaten.'

'True strength is when you build on your failures, not capitalise on your successes.'

'It is not the strongest of the species that survive, nor the most intelligent, but the ones most responsive to change.'

'Strength is a trait that comes from building on other strengths, not from trampling on weakness.'

'If we listen to them when they are five or six or seven years old, they may just listen to us when they are fifteen, sixteen or seventeen.'

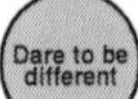

ACTION STEPS

1. Write down a master dream list. List all the things you want to do, be, have, or go to in your lifetime. Pick one dream to do each year with your family.
2. When appraising performance, whether that of a child or a business colleague, start by giving them the highest grade possible. Then ask them to write a letter, as if it was the end of the year, describing what they did to justify the grade.
3. Make sure you pass onto your children the most significant lesson you learned from your father, mother or older person you knew as a child.
4. Take time out to teach your children how to handle money. Help them prepare a simple income and expenditure budget and keep track of it.
5. Take your child or loved one to the place where you work. Let them sit or stand in your place and tell them how you spend your day.
6. Catch your children doing something right – today.
7. Watch one of their favourite television programmes and try to appreciate why they like it.
8. At the next possible opportunity, take a half day. Spend it with those who are important to you.
9. Promise that you will never give up on the relationship with your child or loved one whatever age they are – even if they have left home under a cloud.
10. Make a list of values that are important to you. Ask yourself whether you are effectively passing those onto your child.

13

The Business Market and High Net Worth Clients

This short chapter on the business and high net worth market is intended to whet your appetite. To do the subject justice I would need to write several volumes. Yet, from what I am about to give you, you can make a start, and that's the biggest step most advisers refuse.

At the time of writing this, my company, Forte Global Consulting, is about to embark on a major project to coach financial advisers both in the UK and Far East. It's curious how financial advisers the world over have woken up to the fact that unless they master doing business with SMEs (small to medium size enterprises) and high net worth individuals, they are unlikely to make the 'big league' or become an acknowledged world-class player in the financial services profession.

So why, in financial services, are people more reluctant to play the game with the 'big boys?' In just about every other industry, it's the business market that everyone seems to start with, not work up to.

I think it has a lot to do with the history of financial services, or more accurately put, insurance. One of the all time greats in selling insurance was Frank Bettger. His book on success in selling insurance was an all-time classic.

People like him inspired the multitude who wanted to live the American Dream for real, and those who stood up to be counted invariably did just that. However, from the outset – the selling was almost always done with individuals or their families, not the business itself. Although insurance products were less sophisticated in the 1950s and 1960s and lacked the flexibility and creativity we have today, it was still a market most avoided.

Needless to say, the original world class sales people made their fortunes working quite hard selling in volume. It was often more about quantity rather than quality, and the paradigm seemed to be set in stone.

Only in the last fifteen years, have people really been thinking about working with businesses, and those of us who are doing so wonder why everyone else isn't doing the same. The reality is that the business market place is bigger than the 'domestic' market place – not in terms of numbers of people but in terms of numbers of pounds and dollars available to be earned.

This brief chapter is intended to give a very superficial overview, and hopefully the inspiration to find out more and make some new inroads into an exciting and untapped area of sales potential.

People often ask me the place to start, and I say, 'inside out'. In other words, you have to get your mindset and thinking very clear. Part of the success of individuals in the corporate market comes from self-confidence and a genuine realisation that they can make a big difference to entrepreneurs and business people regardless of the type or size of the business. Having said that, I strongly advise you to start with an SME.

These businesses tend to have no more than a hundred employees and a maximum turnover of around £10m ($15m). They also rarely have any serious financial planning in place and I have yet to meet a business owner in this category who doesn't need what I can offer.

The first challenge is getting in front of your prospect, and I suggest you give some thought as to what you want to say. If you do not yet know how you are going to discuss protecting the business, offering long term investment solutions or simply insuring against this or that, you'll be wasting your time.

Think for a moment. How many products have you bought yourself that deals exclusively with your business needs?

So, if you're not buying your own products, why would anyone else? The answer lies in thinking like a business owner – which by the way you are! You run your own business, albeit within a bigger one if you are tied to a life company. So ask yourself, what do you want?

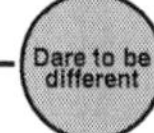

I imagine your list would include:

- ✓ more clients
- ✓ more value for my sales time
- ✓ less stress, more organisation
- ✓ increased turn over
- ✓ lower overheads
- ✓ greater profitability
- ✓ easier ways to sell
- ✓ client loyalty
- ✓ more fun.

So why would any other business owner want anything different? The thing is, I know you are wondering about some of these objectives. I mean, which one of your company's products could you sell to someone wanting client loyalty? Or what about more fun?

So here's the message again. You must start 'inside out'. Get your internal thinking right and what follows will be a more successful approach with plenty of solutions.

The next concept is about being holistic. Businesses want someone who they can call on for a whole variety of reasons, not necessarily someone who is too specialised. And in the financial services industry, many people seek specialisation – for example, those of us who like mortgages, or pension planning, family protection or savings and investment. In the world of business, specialisation can, in fact, mean segregation, confusion and lack of continuity. I am not suggesting that being a generalist is best – what I am saying is if you choose to concentrate on one area of business, make sure that you have access to others who can provide the support you need to offer a total solution.

Being holistic combined with the right mindset will also play a big part. What you call yourself and how you see yourself will be picked up by your business prospect. So if you are a 'business financial planner', you'll be less attractive to a prospect than a 'business growth consultant'. After all, does a business want planning or growth first on their shopping list?

The two most important things for any business are:

✓ growth
✓ profitability.

Turnover is one thing, but profit and growth can, actually, be more easily achieved: cost reduction is an obvious way to increase profit. Again, think this one through.

The next thing to think about is how you can really offer 'the ultimate'. This can be tricky because, if you get it wrong, you end up wasting your time and losing respect in front of your prospect. Get it right and you create your own ultimate business instantly!

The way to make this happen is:

- Read books like *The 'E' Myth* by Michael Gerber – words of wisdom around making small businesses more effective and successful.
- Make notes of the key business ideas and implement them in your own business.
- Pass on these business tips to your prospects with enthusiasm, alongside the process of doing an extensive business fact find.
- Deliver one piece of information each month (you may wish to charge them a fee for this) which would genuinely make a big difference to them and then help them put it into action.
- Ensure any financial planning you do incorporates where they want their business to go in the short, medium and long term. If the products you sell are specifically linked in this way, they are unlikely to be cancelled. Ensure there are simple, explanatory labels on the policy documents associated with their objectives or business goals.
- Network, network and network! (I think you get the idea!) Where possible, link one business with another and keep doing it, often. For example send small businesses lawyers and CPAs (accountants), send property cases to law firms you are helping and send friends looking for a new car to that car dealership owner who has become a client. Networking is a way of planting the seeds for your business in the gardens of others.

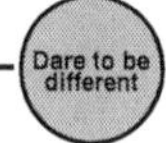

- Set up a way of keeping in touch with all your existing business clients as well as those who haven't come on board yet. This can be done by email.
- Tell everyone you know what you are doing – helping businesses to grow and improve profitability. Get successful testimonies on paper and show new prospects.

I do appreciate in the limited space I have here to deal with this subject, more questions than answers are probably being raised. However, you need to make a start if you intend to take your business in this exciting direction, as I did – and never look back.

Apart from emailing me for more help at sandro@forteglobal.com, I suggest you track down those advisers who you know in the business market and buy them lunch. I am sure they will agree to help put you on the right track.

High net worth clients

The other market worth thinking about is the high net worth market place, where the correct mindset – yours not theirs – is even more critical.

I did say earlier that in business consultancy as a financial adviser, specialising doesn't always help. Where high net worth clients are concerned, there is a form of specialisation needed – specialising in the clients themselves.

To put this into a digestible format, let me tell you a true story of a friend of mine who was a financial adviser in the early eighties. He met up with an old school friend who invited him to his London home. When he arrived at a town house in Belgravia (an expensive part of the city), he was astonished to see this lavish home with a Bentley motor car parked outside. My friend started to doubt whether his old school pal really owned all this opulence, and even wondered if he was a drugs baron! Yet when he enquired what he was up to – he was told he was a photographer.

The school friend went on to say that he wasn't just any old photographer. He decided to do a fundamental course on photography and then specialise on famous faces. In fact that was the name of his business *Famous Faces*. He only took pictures of famous people and if they were not that famous he didn't bother! You can imagine how the word spread – people were ringing him up to see if they were famous enough for his lens to be trained on their face. What a great piece of marketing.

I know someone who did something similar in financial services. He was an American working out of New York. Having failed miserably for several years, he decided he was going to deal only with clients earning more money than he did. Guess what! Within three years, he went from earning $50,000 a year to over $3m.

Though I have famous people as clients, I made a decision to work with businesses as well as well-known high net worth clients, otherwise I would be sorely tempted to deal only with the celebrities who are usually so much fun.

The sad thing is that despite sharing the ideas which could encourage people to enter this market, I still haven't heard of a financial adviser doing this. I suppose it needs courage – but imagine running a business exclusively helping famous people. That's why that photographer had a town house in Belgravia and a Bentley – his rewards for courageous thinking. He got going after tracking down his *first* famous face. Once he had a handful on his books – and his message was out there – the floodgates opened!

The best thing of all about quality business, is the extra time it creates. No work in the evenings or weekends, more family time, spending business time on the golf course or in quality locations, and the joy of dealing with some great people.

Some of my famous clients came from a simple idea given to me by my own personal development coach at the time – the creation of a marketing CD which you send to those famous people you'd like to have as a client. If you think it sounds easy, let me tell you it is – you just have to have the courage to take the first step.

The extraordinary thing is, when you meet these people and ask them if they have a financial adviser, they invariably say 'no'. Even more astounding is when you ask them how many times they have been approached by a financial adviser – and the answer very often is … never. So, what are you waiting for?

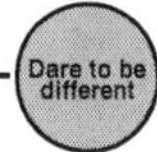

End-of-chapter classic quotes

'Commitment in every activity – especially professional selling – is one of the most important ingredients necessary if you are to succeed and be content in your success. We live by choice, not by chance.'

'Kind words cost little, but accomplish much.'

'Real motivation comes from within.'

'You are what you make of yourself – no one else has that set of raw ingredients.'

'If you ignore your talents, you will live your life in misery, cast out into your own inner darkness.'

'Keep always one dream in your pocket.'

And finally …

'On the last day, you will be asked to account for any good thing you could have enjoyed – and didn't.'

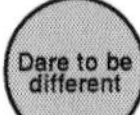

ACTION STEPS

Using this Masterplan, decide on all your personal and professional objectives. Write down what you want from this month, what time off you will have, what issues are causing problems and what standards need to be improved. Use the Masterplan to commit to, and stay in touch with, all the goals you have set whilst reading this book.

This Month's Masterplan

Month

Primary objective

Strategic objective

Personal development

Personality

Prospecting

Irritating items (use pencil here)

1
2
3
4
5
6
7
8
9
10

Wk	Target	Ach

Time off

Improving standards this month

Home

Traits

Self-confidence
Personal effectiveness
Order and Organis'n
Time control
New doors

Happiness
Progress
Backlog
Mindchange
Prospect
Biz=fun

MindChangers

Hotel days this year

Exercise

Do and have this month

Eight objectives	Done?
1	
2	
3	
4	
5	
6	
7	
8	

14

The Future is Here and Now …

I do hope you have found this book a great investment. Right now you will be in one of three possible reader categories.

- Here is a good test of a Category 1 reader – quite simply if you've implemented any ideas since starting the book, then congratulations – you are probably a **'success driver'**. These people waste no time – if any idea is good then they want to use it. Once they see how well the technique works, they'll dip into the book for another and another. The only challenge tends to be that they act first and think second – which can make life more difficult.

- Maybe you are the Category 2 type of reader who makes lots of notes first before taking action. Fair enough. If you fall in this category, you will also have re-read all your notes and probably typed them up. If you've done any of this, you will have a strategy of implementation which you are about to embark on. Well done. You are a **'success planner'**. Sound planning preceding prepared action steps. Provided these people take steps in the way the Success Driver operates, then they will not only see success, but they will also be able to measure it. The downside of being in this category though is the temptation to do too much planning and research rather than taking the necessary actions.

- If you haven't done either of the above, you fall into Category 3. These people have probably another book on success that they will read next. They are constantly striving for answers rather

than driving solutions. They are forever playing the 'Waiting Game'. Waiting for the right time, for the right circumstances, for the right month in the year, for the right weather and so on.

They are in fact highly unlikely to put any of the ideas in this book into action – governed by the little voice in their head constantly chatting away and telling them what not to do rather than to action the things they know in their heart that they should be doing.

These people are called **'Success Saboteurs'**. They commit gross acts of self-sabotage on themselves, and have probably done so for most of their lives. There is a good chance that their parents were not particularly successful in their lives either. And I don't mean they don't have good careers – it's just that they never became outrageously successful in what they did and certainly nothing note-worthy or extraordinary. Which is why you may be following the same path. Doing better than your father and mother can be considered by some as a lack of respect, and deep down success saboteurs want to avoid being more successful than them at all costs.

So, here are the real ways to maximise the contents of this book and dramatically change your level of success in business and life itself.

☑ **Choose to ignore any negative 'internal dialogue'.**

☑ **Plan your steps by reviewing notes and the chapters of this book.**

☑ **Take action today and *persist* with *consistency* day by day until you get to where you want to be, choosing not to make any excuses as to why you haven't arrived there yet.**

Many years ago, I remember hearing the story of 'The Black Door', which always stuck in my mind. It tells of the nature of human thinking and how most of us are choosing what we do not want rather than what we do.

The story is about a war in the Middle East over one hundred years ago where a general of the Persian Army was brought an enemy spy. It was common practice to put spies to death without question, yet the general was a man of some compassion and took a slightly different view of how to deal with this particular individual.

In fact, he gave the spy a choice. He could be put against a wall and shot by firing squad or he could be pushed through the 'Black Door'. It was up to the spy which fate he wished to bring upon himself.

It didn't take long for the spy to come to a decision. No one had yet passed through the ominous and mysterious Black Door. Like most spies given this choice, he chose the firing squad. It was the known outcome rather than the fear of the Black Door and the unknown. The general stared at his boots in dismay as the firing squad was assembled and subsequently the sentence carried out.

One of the aides of the general had to ask the question.

'Sir, what does lie beyond the Black Door?'

'Freedom,' he retorted, *'and I have yet to meet a man brave enough to go through it.'*

Sad as it is, I see so many people who seek the firing squad over the Black Door. Ask yourself the question – is there a Black Door you can choose to go through that you're avoiding right now? Or are you putting yourself up against the wall and facing a firing squad time and time again?

You can now do something about it.

Whatever category you're in, make sure you go back and pick out all the best ideas from this book. Make sure you have listed them on the ACTION LIST pages at the ends of the chapters, categorising them as A, B or Z.

'A' actions are for immediate deployment, 'B' actions are to put into your diary for deployment within the next 1-6 months and 'Z' means something worth noting that you will review after all the 'A' and 'B' actions have been completed.

What follows is a 12-point 'Big Picture' summary of everything we've covered in this book, in a few simple concept sentences.

1. **Activity:** motion in a set direction that builds and builds in the direction you seek. Ideally your planned activity should be on a daily basis and reviewed regularly. For example, if you want to write a book, start writing fifty words each and every day – and such planned activity will deliver you a completed manuscript, guaranteed.

2. **Regime:** a daily diet of good habits that brings stability to your being. If you have no regime, you are not working a plan which means you are travelling in a rowing boat without oars.

3. **Escape to freedom:** a detailed Master Plan or blueprint of your route to the final winning post. Some people say they have the plan in their mind. Sorry, I can't accept this. This plan should be written down and detailed. Written goals are one hundred times more powerful than 'remembered' goals. Remembered goals, by the way, should not be confused with MindChangers.

4. **Action now:** the taking of immediate action secures your future results. Thought plus action always creates a result. If you are a results producer, you are most likely to create enough outcomes to secure the success you seek.

5. **Future now:** the act of playing out what you want now, guarantees its future arrival. Act as if what you want is around you today. T J Watson, the man behind the IBM success story, started in a tiny office that looked and felt like part of a multi-million dollar company from day one. How could he not be on track in subsequently creating it?

6. **Inner image:** polish up who you are and inspire yourself to new heights. If you don't like yourself, have confidence in your abilities and do everything possible to consistently improve your

mind and body – otherwise, how can others have trust and confidence in you? How you appear to others fuels how you ultimately view yourself. Look 'the business' and get the winning feeling.

7. **MindChangers:** turn the keys in your mind and open the door to all possibilities. These amazing tools have been responsible for winners over the last sixty years. Can you risk ignoring them?

8. **Order and organisation:** create a positive foundation and platform for continuous success. How can you be successful working from an untidy office, a paper filled desk, from a dirty car or in scruffy clothes? The things around you, especially your environment, say much about who you are and influence who you will become. It also makes you infinitely more effective and hence more likely to succeed. Remember – if in doubt, throw it out. Less is always more!

9. **New horizons:** doing what others refuse to do puts you at the top of *The Success Waiting List*. You know what you should do, even if your little voice says otherwise. Simply do what you least want to do, and do the worst things (that you need to do) first…and notice how much progress you start to make.

10. **Practise:** being an expert in your chosen arena automatically creates multi opportunities, many of which could be beyond your wildest dreams. But, remember the importance of a complete service.

11. **Fear:** (False Evidence Appearing Real) fear is life gauging your commitment, not to mention courage. Time to go through the Black Door?

12. **The Concept of Now:** Enjoy the moment and you'll have fewer regrets. Often we are too busy thinking of other things to consider living a more balanced existence. If you are playing with your

child or spending quality time with your partner, but with your mind on business matters, you are probably missing the point as to what success is really all about!

And finally … remember this … always.

I don't have the answers to your life – you do.

Somewhere inside you is the potential for greatness. Choose to find it, or leave your unlimited potential behind you in a wooden box. It's your decision.

You've taken a big step in finishing this book, and you've displayed the first and most important critical success factor – *consistency*. May I wish you amazing success on your journey in life, and outstanding results for everything that you passionately desire.